FUEL
Your Life

A 4-point Practice
To Spiritual Awakening

Written and illustrated by
GINA CHARLES

Gina Charles Publishing
www.ginacharles.com
New York

Copyright © 2015 Gina Charles
All rights reserved
Published in the United States of America
Original cover design and illustrations by Gina Charles

ISBN-13: 978-0-9861138-1-9

All rights reserved. No part of this book may be reproduced or transmitted in any form or by any means, electronic or mechanical, including photocopying, recording or by any information storage and retrieval system, without the prior written permission from the copyright owner, author and publisher.

The scanning, uploading, and distribution of this book via the Internet, excluding authorized electronic purchase and download, or via any and all other means without the written permission of the copyright owner, author and publisher is illegal and punishable by law. Your support of the author's rights is appreciated.

This book was written to provide conceptual information. It is distributed with the understanding that the publisher and author are not engaged in rendering legal, medical or any other such professional services. If legal, medical or other expert assistance is required, the services of a competent professional should be sought. It is not the purpose of this book to reiterate conceptual information that is otherwise available, but instead to reintroduce it, complement and amplify it. You are encouraged to read any or all related available material, and tailor the information to your individual needs, if at all. This book contains information based on personal revelations and spiritual growth of the author, complete and as accurate as possible, and is current up to the publishing date. The purpose of this book is to present contemplative information and is at the discretion of the reader.

For
Anthony Charles
and
Raul Garcia

*There is another way to
have this human adventure.*
-Gina Charles

CONTENTS

INTRODUCTION 8

PART ONE: WHAT'S THIS ALL ABOUT? 10
Realization 14
Thought 20
The Human Experience 34

PART TWO: FUEL YOUR LIFE 42
Flow Emotion 47
Unconditional Acceptance 55
The Eyewitness 60
Lucidity 69
Practicing The Practice 75

PART THREE: FIFTY SHADES OF AWAKENING..81
Addiction 82
Anger 88
Anxiety 92
Attachment 95
Bullying 98
Change 101
Creativity 104
Control 107

Depression	110
Desire	114
Disconnect	118
Fear	121
Food	128
Forgiveness	135
Freedom	140
Future	144
Gratitude	147
Grief	151
Guilt	155
Happiness	160
Heartbreak	166
Hurt	169
Illness	173
Inspiration	176
Joy	179
Life Purpose	182
Loneliness	188
Love	191
Meditation	195
Money	198
Overwhelm	202
Past	206
Peace	209
Powerless	213
Presence	217
Problems	220
Procrastination	225
Regret	229

Relationships 232
Resistance 235
Sadness 238
Scarcity 244
Shame 247
Stress 251
Stuck 255
Success 259
Surrender 262
Vulnerability 266
Worry 271
Worth 275

PART FOUR: JUMP 280
Empowerments At A Glance 284

INTRODUCTION

Beyond The Words

A hungry man told me he was starving. I made him a sandwich. Others made him sandwiches. The hungry man collected up the sandwiches, and died of starvation.

To experience the effects of food, we must eat, and digest it. To experience the effects of spiritual knowledge, we must eat and digest it. Collecting spiritual information is like collecting sandwiches, and then starving to death.

Digesting spiritual knowledge is to go beyond the analytical or conceptual understanding. It is to go beyond the words, into a visceral knowing, from a perspective previously unseen. This is also known as a realization. The portal to Conscious expansion, or spiritual awakening, is a series of inner shifts, or realizations.

The Real You

What's really happening underneath the people, places and things in our lives, is this journey back to Self. This is not to imply that our purpose is to serve and embellish the mind-made identity. Rather it is to infer that the real you, lies just outside of that mind-made identity. Who are you apart from your descriptions and beliefs?

FUEL Your Life

Over time, my efforts toward self-growth have evolved into a four-point, foundational practice. I flow emotion, exercise unconditional acceptance, am the eyewitness to thought and emotion, and I practice lucidity.

Practicing these four perspectives in my everyday life, has been the precursor to powerful realizations. These realizations have not only offered a way out of pain and suffering, but have also offered the clarity of a new way to have this human adventure.

FUEL Your Life is a 4-point practice, offering pocket-sized, authentic living perspectives that can be applied to anyone's everyday life. It is for anyone, anytime, anywhere. Have your sandwich, and eat it too.

Fifty Shades Of Awakening

A painful situation, is a realization that hasn't happened yet. The fifty shades listed in this book, stand as an open invitation for realization. The shades are our everyday life experiences, such as anger, stress, relationships, even gratitude and joy.

Each shade, or experience, is looked at via FUEL Your Life. Let's go beyond the words, and experience the inner shift of realization. I'm not asking you to believe a word I say. I'm inviting you to try it for yourself. There is another way to have this human adventure.

PART ONE

WHAT'S THIS ALL ABOUT?

*If we are facing in the right direction,
all we have to do is keep on walking.
-Buddhist Proverb*

I live as if life is a message to me. If something hurts, it is either untrue, or I am in resistance. When this realization rises up, pain and suffering fall away. Imagine how different this human experience would have been, having been taught that nifty little trick as a child.

We spend time chasing a certain kind of life, when we're not present for the one we already have. For it is the life that I have, in all its unbiased isness, that points me in the direction of my highest good.

Carrots And Carts

When I realized that I am the one who is responsible for my life experience, and the only one who can save or enlighten me, I decided to scrape together enough self-worth to show up for myself. Realizing that I was worth the effort, was the carrot that I dangled in front of my baggage-laden cart.

Until I experienced this realization, my thinking mind wove all kinds of knight-in-shining-armor stories. I looked outside of myself for something to swoop me up and get me to the safe and happy place; a job, a move, a project, a person. Some knights in shining armor were handsome, others rushed in as chocolate cake. Then there were the knights, that at the hint of my despair, would drop into protective formation to light my cigarette.

My life was trying to tell me something. It was showing me what I believed about it. It was offering sign posts toward my best, authentic life. I was too busy listening to the fear-based guesswork of the thinking mind. We don't have to believe that life is fair, to take responsibility for where we are right now. We don't have to wait until life squeezes so hard, that it feels difficult to breathe. We don't have to wait to be happy.

Authentic Living

It is possible to see beyond misunderstanding and resistance, and to wake up out of pain and suffering. We can step into peace and possibility, and discover passion and purpose. This book is about finding your power, and learning how to live it.

We long to put down our baggage, and empty our closets. We want to be comfortable and secure, connecting to this human adventure wholeheartedly. Free to be whoever we really are, outside of who we think we should or could be. We crave passion and dream of life purpose. We long to honor our truths like we're not doing anything wrong. We long to love ourselves enough to live authentically.

*The life of my dreams is
an authentic life experience.*

If I don't experience an authentic life, I won't experience the life I've been longing for. The life of my dreams is an authentic life experience. Life can never be as good, as when lived authentically. When I find, face and honor my truths, I flow with the current of my highest good. This is authentic living. For that I must get real with myself, come clean, kiss honesty on the mouth and surrender into the unknown. It makes a thinking mind want to run screaming in resistance.

Filters Or Freedom

A premise through which I view life, is a filter. Today I may see everything through the filter of stress. Tomorrow I may view life through the filter of fear, or worthlessness. Viewing and participating in life through filters, skews and limits my life experience.

The greatest filter of all is the mind-made identity. We live our lives in service to it. If our minds value intelligence, we study. If we live in fear, we hide or fight. If we want to be accepted, loved, or successful, we cater to cultivating an accomplished identity.

> *Ironically, protecting and enhancing the story of the mind-made identity, becomes the very limitation in which we live.*

When we don't recognize this dynamic, we end up living our lives going back and forth between what feels good, and what feels bad. Ironically, protecting and enhancing the story of the mind-made identity, becomes the very limitation in which we live.

It is possible to experience life directly, without the filter of the mind-made identity, or unnecessary thought. This is the space of authenticity. Here, I am lucid. I am present, outside of a story line, in the comfort and peace of unconditional acceptance. In lucidity, I have found healing, serendipity, and real joy. Not that thought-made, synthetic joy that the thinking mind manufactures. I go from contorting myself trying to make change happen, to noticing change happen *for* me. In this state, I see that pain and suffering are optional.

Going beyond the logical understanding into an innate knowing, is what this whole adventure is about. It's not about *saying*, it's about *seeing* for yourself. When I began to view life with my mind's mouth shut, reality appeared, and changed everything.

REALIZATION

The Magic Ingredient

*Realization is the digestion
of spiritual information.*

What's the magic ingredient, without which I cannot awaken? Realization. Realization is the digestion of spiritual information. I collect up my sandwiches, but can never be satiated until I eat and digest them.

If you're reading this book, you've probably already amassed a degree of spiritual knowledge, although that's not a prerequisite. This book is not meant to add any more spiritual information to your pile, without offering a way to go beyond the conceptual understanding. What's the use of collecting more spiritual knowledge if I don't live it?

*Realization is the difference between struggling
to create myself, and becoming mySelf.*

Realization is to go beyond the words. It takes me from conceptual understanding, to an intuitive, or intrinsic knowing. Realization is the difference between struggling to create myself, and becoming mySelf. Realization bridges the gap between searching for the life of my dreams, and living the life of my dreams.

Trouble's Treasures

The construct is so benevolent, that it will never cease offering us ways back to our Selves.

Life offers us opportunities for realizations that keep us moving toward our highest good. We either recognize them, or we don't. If we don't, the opportunity, sometimes known as a "problem," comes back until we do. Different places, different faces, same unopened realizations. The construct is so benevolent, that it will never cease offering us ways back to our Selves. Back to authentic peace and joy.

Move Over

If I wanted to move something from here to there, my mind believes that it would have to find a way to pick it up, slide it, kick it, somehow move it from one place to another. Similarly, if I wanted to experience something move inside of myself, like a spiritual shift, the thought is that I would have to find a way to do or make that shift happen.

*There is a difference between
moving something, and being moved.*

While I can pick up this pencil and move it over there, I cannot make an inner shift, or realization happen. There is a difference between moving something, and being moved. Realization is the equivalent of being moved. The thing to do is to mentally move over, and get out of your own way. The less mental gridlock, the more available I am to realization.

Luring Realization

Realization may not be something that the thinking mind can do, but it is something that it can intend, allow and invite. Practicing FUEL Your Life is an open invitation for realization. When I'm lucid, acceptant, and witnessing thought and emotion as I experience it, I put myself where realization can find me.

The Creamy Middle

If I cracked open a realization what would I find? What is the thing that realization offers? Truth. The cream-filled middle of realization is my truth. What exactly is my truth? My truth is what is, in its untainted form. It's the reality of a situation apart from my mind's version of it. When I see the isness of a situation, I no longer see truth in my anger, sadness, or fear. Pain subsequently dissipates.

Truth Is Wordless

*Realization is to experience a
wordless, spontaneous knowing.*

A realization can be put into words, but it does not originate there. There is a sudden recognition of something previously unnoticed, and it resonates in an unlearned way. Realization is to experience a wordless, spontaneous knowing. It is the sudden clarity of truth. Truth is wordless.

*A realization is a spontaneous
recognition of a new perspective. It is
not a story about a new perspective.*

A realization is undeniable. The information emerges in one block of silent knowledge. A realization is a spontaneous recognition of a new perspective. It is not a story about a new perspective. Although I would use words to explain the realization to someone else, words and thoughts are not necessary for me to know and understand this information in its entirety.

Realization is the portal to awakening. It is the supersonic tonic for Conscious expansion. Many realizations are regarding the self-made identity, the personality, the ego. One could say that with each realization of truth, a tiny piece of the self-made identity dissolves.

A Taste To Acquire

There is no wonder why self-growth is the road less traveled. It can be difficult at times. Facing the truth is hard for a thinking mind. Who wants to recognize themselves acting like someone they believe they are not? Who wants to realize that they were mistaken? A thinking mind doesn't like that. The mind doesn't like anything that curtails the ongoing internal dialog, or dismantles its own identity.

On the other hand, some truths are finger-licking good. Like the ones we recognize when our minds pipe down long enough, to see all the benevolence and abundance that is already present in our lives. Experience tells me that the truth that tastes the worst, produces the most empowering blast of personal power.

So the question is, what will I choose for myself? Will I step up to my truths for the realization of authentic growth and freedom? Or will I continue to talk about life from behind the shield of overlooked thought and old programming, and then have the nerve to wonder why I feel stuck or lost? No matter which way I pour it, sweet or sour, acquiring a taste for truth is highly advantageous.

That Changes Everything

My mind likes to differentiate realization into three categories: smaller ah-ha moments, medium-sized realizations, and the holy-cow-that-changes-everything epiphany. The baby of the bunch is what I call an *ah-ha* moment. An ah-ha moment feels like a light bulb going off in my head. Then there's the medium-sized realization, which I boringly refer to as a *realization*. This feels like getting my hair blown back.

Finally, I like to reserve the word *epiphany* for the realizations that make me feel like the earth just got pulled out from under me, and I'm dangling upside down by one ankle. Thankfully, it is within those epiphanic moments that clarity wraps me in a loving embrace, and cradles me as I absorb my truth and freedom.

The ultimate realization is becoming aware that I am not my story, changed or otherwise.

We have all gone through things that have changed us in some way. Our authentic realizations of truth, change us for the better. They make us stronger and wiser. The ultimate realization is becoming aware that I am not my story, changed or otherwise.

THOUGHT

*Thought is the limitation within
which I have this human experience.*

The Box

Thought is the limitation within which I have this human experience. At first, that may be a slippery concept to grasp. Beyond the understanding that I can think, and fall immersed into thought, is the concept that I can step out of thought. We fall into thought much like falling into a pond and being completely submerged under water. The difference is, we don't realize when we are submerged in thought.

As long as I'm experiencing life from inside the box of thoughts, stories, beliefs, and mental conjecture, my happiness will be a temporary candy coating. Jumping out of the box is equivalent to gaining lucidity, or waking up to being present in the moment, outside of unneeded thought. It is to be awake, or present within the silence of the mind. Jumping out of the box, gives my higher Self a direct connection to this playground we call life. This is the space from which authentic change and elation manifests.

There Is Only This Or That

I offer you the concept of two states of being. There are two ways in which to have this human experience. I am either lucid, present in mental quietude, or I am immersed in and believing unmonitored thought.

Living identified in the mental assessment of life, offers a perpetual susceptibility to pain and suffering.

While lucid, I enter the state of infinite possibilities, and have a much better connection to my own Guidance, the real me, the keeper of serendipity and joy. Conversely, while entangled in thought, I am the puppet, reacting to life with memorized behavior. Living identified in the mental assessment of life, offers a perpetual susceptibility to pain and suffering.

Is It Live, Or Is It Memorized?

Instinct, guidance, and intuition are outside of thought. Experiencing life with my shields down, or with thought at a minimum, gives me greater access to those innate resources. I'm living live, outside of the boundary of limitation.

Are you on autopilot, reacting to life, or are you awake and aware, responding to life?

Learned, or reactive behavior is inside of thought. When we are submerged in thought, we are running on autopilot. On autopilot, the same thoughts, patterns and behaviors produce more of the same results. I'm living within the boundaries of what's memorized. Are you on autopilot, reacting to life, or are you awake and aware, responding to life?

Snow Globe Of The Frontal Lobe

The thinking mind is like a snow globe. The tiny specs of glitter that float around inside are like thoughts, beliefs and stories. There are stories about who we think we are, our life experience, and everything in it.

The snow globe of the frontal lobe pumps out evaluations, judgements, and opinions. This is the kind of thinking that is unnecessary. The kind of thinking that my life does not depend on. This type of thinking becomes the bubble through which I try to live my life.

By associating to, and believing unassessed thought, we become submersed in it. We are unaware, wondering why happiness seems like such a hard task. In the meantime, reality waits just outside.

When thought is the foreground of life, reality becomes the background.

We are unconscious, sleepwalking inside of our stories. When we shake our globes, stirring up these stories, we find ourselves in a mental storm. Lost in a storm that is made up of no more than thought. It's not until we realize where we are, that we can get out. When thought is the foreground of life, reality becomes the background. To live as our true Selves, outside of the globe of thought, we must switch states. In lucidity, the clarity of truth becomes the forefront of my experience, and thought becomes the background. This is authentic living.

The Pond

The Pond is an analogy that I presented in my first book, *Shift Happens, A Layperson's Guide To Awakening*. The pond has three sections. The inner circle of the pond is the feel-bad swim. The outer circle of the pond is the feel-good swim. The outermost section is the shore. The water, both feel-good and feel-bad sections, represent thought. The shore represents Lucidity, or being present outside of inessential thought.

We spend our lives swimming back and forth between the feel-good and feel-bad waters of life, splashing around in unconsciousness and misconception. Both feel-good and feel-bad experiences are temporary. Living submersed in thought leaves us susceptible to the currents of unconsciousness, which means we're going with a flow we have no real influence over.

It is when I realize that there is something else, that I begin to experience Conscious expansion. To be standing on the shore, represents being lucid and free of inordinate thought. This is the place from which I may observe the events of my life, that used to cause pain and suffering, without being affected in the same way. This is the place from which my truths are not distorted or skewed.

In The Valley Of Faux Mercy

I value the power of positive thinking. Until I can step outside of, or turn thought off completely, I can choose positive thought. If I'm going to live in a story, I'll at least try to make it a good one.

That said, be leery not to wander too far into The Valley of Faux Mercy. The thinking mind likes this place, as it perpetuates thinking. Whether I am submersed in negative thought, or I am submersed in positive thought, I am still submersed in thought. It's all still thought. Negative thought hurts right away, and positive thought has the potential to bring temporary relief. The ebb and flow between the two allows me to rest just long enough to endure another struggle. Around, and around I go.

Using the power of positive thinking helps to turn my ship around. Happy is better than sad any day. But there's something more, something even better. Use positive thought to get you to the feel-good swim. That's one step closer to getting to the shore of lucidity.

Patterns, Programs And Puppets

Unnoticed thought produces emotion and behavior that create the limiting patterns in which we live.

Our brains learn by repetition. When we repeat something, it is memorized within the electrical activity in the brain. Since typing has become hard-wired in my brain, I am able to type quickly and effortlessly. Along with activity, behavior can be memorized as well. Although my mind can learn how to type, or dance, it can also learn self-sabotage, defensiveness, and fear. Unnoticed thought produces emotion and behavior that create the limiting patterns in which we live.

How much thought am I really having? Is it incessant? Is it accurate? Is it helpful and inspiring, or is it debilitating and self-sabotaging? Am I rerunning old thoughts and beliefs that no longer serve me? How much thought is being used as a helpful tool, and how much is inessential to my survival?

When I have and believe thought without noticing it, I am the puppet, and unsupervised thought is the puppeteer.

How would I even know what kind of thought I'm having? Do I really notice the thoughts that are romping through the mind? No, most often we do not. When I have and believe thought without noticing it, I am the puppet, and unsupervised thought is the puppeteer.

> *I have the power to break the pattern in which my reactions fire, turning me into a puppet of resistance and misunderstanding.*

I did not control the circumstances that lent themselves to the programming of my formative years. I am, however, responsible for that programming today. I possess the power to deprogram. I have the power to break the pattern in which my reactions fire, turning me into a puppet of resistance and misunderstanding.

Please Sir, I'll Have No More

The thinking mind has two priorities. The first is to think, and the other is to enhance the mind-made identity. Make no mistake, the thinking mind will take every opportunity to do what it does best, think. In a way, you can't blame it. It's only doing what it was made to do.

The eyes blink, the heart beats and the lungs respire. If my eyes are blinking excessively, it is because of the dust in the air, strong light, or smoke that is burning my eyes. The excess blinking would be necessary.

> *Surplus thought anesthetizes you to life.*

Excessive thought, however intoxicating, is not necessary to my well-being or existence. Unwarranted thought eventually produces bad feelings. The bad feelings are the messengers, the sign posts, the alarms, that we are engulfed in gratuitous thought. Surplus thought anesthetizes you to life. Feeling bad is the Universe's way of resuscitating us.

While I can't blame my thinking mind for doing what it was made to do, I can awaken from being submersed in its excesses. When I practice lucidity the mind begins to cut back on surplus thought.

Once Removed

What effect does surplus thought have on my day-to-day life experience? Being free of unneeded thought versus being engulfed in it, is equivalent to living life authentically versus living life once removed.

Excess thought becomes the static that prevents me from hearing my own Guidance.

Being unaware that I am buried in indiscriminate thought, stories, and beliefs, perpetuates the filter. The filter of thought is the obstruction to inner peace, and the Joy that I am. Excess thought becomes the static that prevents me from hearing my own Guidance. The worst thing that can happen is unnoticed, unexamined thinking.

There's an absence of inner ease and security when I'm inadvertently existing inside the bubble of thought. I am living life as if. When I unwittingly fall into thought, those very thoughts become the smoke through which I try to enjoy this life experience.

> *When you realize that you are the*
> *eyewitness to your stories, as opposed to*
> *living submersed in them, you are Awake.*

The thoughts themselves are not detrimental. Thoughts are more like fluttering butterflies, clouds passing across the sky, or leaves drifting down a river. The detriment of thought lies in attaching to and believing it. When you realize that you are the eyewitness to your stories, as opposed to living submersed in them, you are awake. Welcome home.

Parting The Sea Of Thought

Even if we don't always notice our thoughts, eventually we do notice an onslaught of mental activity. It's uncomfortable, to say the least. What can we do when thought is blowing around like a twister in a corn field?

Look at thought objectively. Look at thought in its separate isness. In our daily lives, we don't make the distinction between the oxygen-filled atmosphere, and ourselves. We don't notice it. Much like we do not make the distinction between thought and self. I am not the atmosphere, I am in the atmosphere. I am not thought, but sometimes I live within it, and do not notice.

How do I slice the atmosphere of thought? What can I do to slow down the momentum, and quiet the mind? Placing my attention, without mental comment, on my breathing or my own heartbeat helps to take some of the wind out of the thinking mind's sails. Each time I notice another thought, I let it drift by and just keep bringing myself back to another peaceful, slow, deep breath. A few minutes of this and the thinking mind begins to get the message, and slows down. Thought is not the boss, my wordless Awareness is.

Getting lucid is equivalent to parting the sea of thought.

There is also another little tactic I use when thought is rambling relentlessly. I picture parting thought and holding it at bay, much like Moses parted the Red Sea. I kid you not. I mentally hold up my mind's little hands and stop thought in its tracks. Getting lucid is equivalent to parting the sea of thought.

I pay attention to the silence in the head, and acknowledge any sounds, smells or sensations of the present moment, without evaluation. I do this for as many moments as I can, exercising my mind's might, before I notice thought leaking back in. The key is to make sure that my focus does not attach to a thought. This process takes as long as it does, from a few seconds to however long you're able to revel in lucidity.

A couple of rounds of Parting The Sea Of Thought makes a big difference. Thought recedes, and I resume identifying with the ever-present inner peace. If at first you don't succeed, please do try, try agin. As with any new skill, you'll warm up to it, and before long you'll be a pro. Sometimes, you just have to part the sea.

The Metacognitive Gatekeeper

Some thoughts are laced with reason, conjecture and supposition. If I observe these thoughts and recognize them as unnecessary, I could send them packing. If I'm not witnessing my thoughts, they traipse right past the gate, and get accepted and believed before I even get a change to get a good look at them.

What's one of the most empowering things I can do for myself? I don't need any tools, I can do it anywhere, at anytime, and it's free. I can be the eyewitness to thought and emotion.

Something Much Greater

Thought is part of my gear. I am geared up in this body I call a vehicle, with this invaluable operating system called the thinking mind. I am not my vehicle or my operating system. I am something much greater.

THE HUMAN EXPERIENCE

- On -	- Off -
- Conscious	- unconscious
- aware	- unaware
- outside of thought	- submersed in thought
- lucid	- sleepwalking
- authentic living	- inauthentic living
- Self	- self
- higher Self / Soul	- thought / identity / ego
- reality	- mind's version of reality
- outside of pain and suffering	- perpetual potential for pain and suffering
- feel good	- feel bad

This Or That

This is the part where I talk about the crux of this human adventure. This is what it all boils down to. Metaphorically, I see two circles on the floor. I can stand inside this one, or I can stand inside that one. All I have to do is to remember that there are two choices. We all have two choices, or two circles in which to stand.

There you are, standing inside one of your two circles. Let's say that you have no idea that you have two circles, two states of being, two different places to stand. If I started pointing to your unoccupied circle, but you believe that you are already occupying the only space there is to occupy, then I just seem crazy to you.

> *There are two ways to have this human adventure.*

I'm no crazier than the next guy. I just see two circles. When I stand in one circle, I'm off, sleepwalking and reacting to life. When I stand in the other circle, I'm on, connected and responding to life. Moving back and forth between the circles is Conscious expansion, spiritual awakening, human evolution. There are two ways to have this human adventure.

The Duality Of The Human Condition

I am in either one of the two circles, or states of being, at any given moment of my life. Every life experience I have fits into one of these two categories, here in this place of duality, whether I recognized it or not.

I am either Conscious or unconscious. I am aware, or unaware. I am in the proverbial box, or I am outside of it. What exactly does this mean? It means that I am either lucid, present in the moment and free of unnecessary thinking, or I am submerged in and believing my thoughts and stories. I am either "on" or "off."

The On State

"On" is the state in which I live when I'm awake, aware, or lucid. It is a space of Consciousness, with a capital C. When I experience life here, outside of the bubble of thought, I am having an unfiltered, authentic life experience. I'm perceiving life outside of, or without the shield of the mental commentary. The "on" state is infused with peace, ease, and self-kindness.

When I'm awake and aware, the mental narrative is at a minimum. Here I have a much better shot at hearing the whispers of my own intuition. In this space, the flow of creativity runs freely for the taking. I connect directly to the people, places and things in my life. I'm outside of memorized behavior, free to respond spontaneously and authentically. This is the state of unlimited possibility.

On-Thought

"On" thoughts are instinctual or intuitive. They produce neutral or feel-good feelings. These thoughts are simple, and telling. I can feel the truth of the thought. Other thought in this category includes technical thought, like driving a car, sending an email, or writing computer code. This category of thought is devoid of thinking that enhances the self-made identity, or thought that is laced with subjective preferences.

The Off State

I'm "off" when I'm unaware, or unconscious. I am having thought and believing it, simultaneously. When I experience life through the veil of thought, I am having a filtered life experience. I am living life once removed.

The reality of life is drowned out by the garrulity of unconsciousness. I don't feel my inner promptings, or notice the messenger of emotion. I don't notice these sign posts, because I am focused on the string of extraneous thought parading through the mind.

While sleepwalking, I am a servant to erroneous programming. The programming that causes me to react rather than respond to life. Not only am I flying deaf and blind, but I don't realize it. When I'm "off" I'm living an inauthentic life, where my beliefs and learned behavior call all the shots. This is the state of limited possibility.

Off-Thought

"Off" thoughts are the thoughts that are on parade in the continual mental assessment. You can spot these thoughts by some of their tell-tail signs. You will notice that most of these thoughts cater to strengthening, improving, augmenting, enriching or adding to the self-made identity.

These thoughts are intertwined with opinion, preference, judgement, evaluation, prediction, speculation and conjecture. Another indication of indiscriminate thought is that it is quite often fear-based. Finally, the best indication of an "off" thought, is its resulting bad feeling.

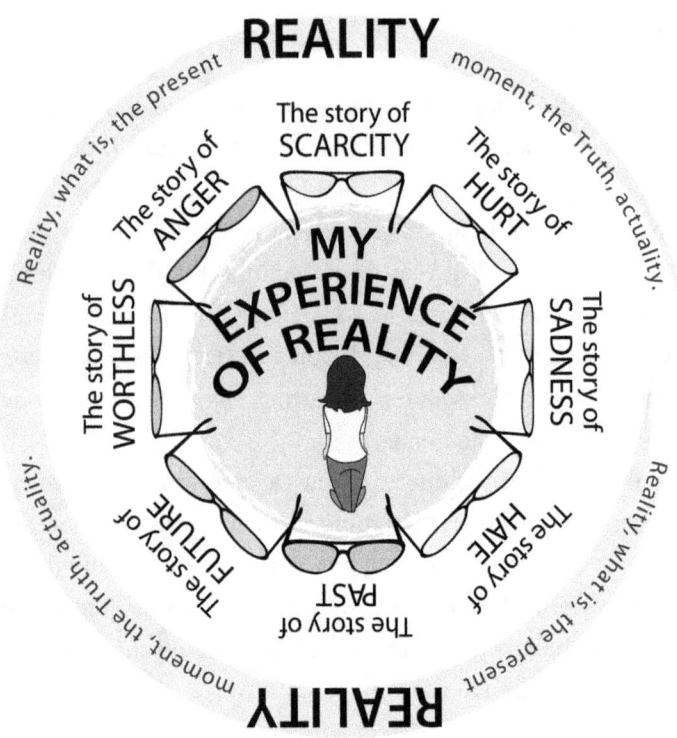

Your Reality, Actual Reality

Along with having access to two states of being, I also have access to two types of reality. There is the thinking mind's experience of reality, and there is actual reality.

Clarity is blurred by my beliefs.

My stories skew my view of actual reality. It's like looking at life through purple-colored glasses. Everything I see will have a purple tinge to it. Similarly, looking at life through my stories of sadness, anger, and fear, will tinge everything in my life with the experience of sadness, anger and fear. Clarity is blurred by my beliefs.

Practicing any of the four perspectives of FUEL Your Life, helps me to recognize when I'm wearing a feel-bad story like a pair of bad sunglasses. As the eyewitness, I catch the thoughts as they come up and recognize them as unnecessary, untrue, or just plain sour. In removing my story-colored glasses, I venture into the space that's rife with miracles that have my name on them.

The End Of Daze

Every moment of our waking lives we are in either one state or the other. If you are experiencing the frequent movement back and forth, between the states of awareness and unawareness, you are awakening. It doesn't matter how many times you fall asleep into thought. It's all about waking up. In recognizing this, we find ourselves on the threshold of the next stage of human evolution. The final frontier is inward.

Me, Myself and I

Which am I? Confusing as it may be, I am not my self-made identity. I am not the personality who calls herself Gina, a woman, a mother, an artist, a friend. This is a learned description, not who I really am. The real me is the energy that's riding around in this meat-suit, made of amnesia and nerve endings.

It is not, "I think, therefore I am."
It is, I Am, therefore I can think.

I am not the roles I play. I am not the thoughts I think. I am not the beliefs my reasoning formulates. It is not, "I think, therefore I am." It is, I Am, therefore I can think. I am the nameless, silent Thing in the background, aware of thought, and the illusions of this dream. When this knowing is held within my awareness, I am awake. I am open to the flow of the Universe. I am That which is, Consciousness. I am Life itself.

Awakening is the process of
becoming yourself, not creating yourself.

Awakening is not about creating yourself by adding to the self-made identity, but rather a shedding of what is not necessary. Awakening is the process of becoming yourself, not creating yourself.

Providence Lives Between Thought

When I unwittingly recede into thought, feel-bad comes to the rescue. Fear, in one of its many disguises, pops up to kick me in the pants, sometimes repeatedly, to alert me to my own unconsciousness. Discomfort gives me a little squeeze so that I may awaken to realize that I'm out here unnecessarily trying to prove myself.

When I am in the peaceful space outside of, or in between thought, I feel as if life rises up to meet me. I've noticed consistently, that when I experience life in this way, providence taps me on the shoulder and gives me a little hug. I experience a realization, I get a great idea, I slide into the creative flow, or a grand solution falls into my lap.

I usually end up experiencing an invigorating state of being. This is living life directly, authentically, without the barrier, veil, filter of excessive and nonessential thought. Everything seems to be exactly the same, and yet everything seems completely and wonderfully different.

PART TWO

FUEL YOUR LIFE

A FOUR-POINT PRACTICE
THAT IS A LIVING MEDITATION

FUEL Your Life

F - **F**low emotion
U - Accept **U**nconditionally
E - Be the **E**yewitness
L - Step into **L**ucidity

Waking Up

If deep down inside I believe that I do not deserve a life that's easy and enjoyable, the moment that I recognize an easy and enjoyable experience, thought will sabotage it. The thinking mind will douse it in untruths, until it creates the experience of its painful belief.

*How can I wake myself up,
if I don't realize that I'm asleep?*

If that's not bad enough, thought conveniently does not notice itself. I'm sleepwalking inside of unmonitored thought, wondering why I'm having such a tough time. This brings us to the question that will change your life experience as you know it. How can I wake myself up, if I don't realize that I'm asleep?

The practices of FUEL Your Life, support you in waking yourself up and staying awake. We can awaken into lucidity repeatedly, until we begin to see through the veil of our misunderstandings, and our programming rewires itself. We can enjoy the dream without it becoming a nightmare. It's possible to see through our discomfort, stagnation and unhappiness. We can wake up to our purpose, the ride of our lives.

New View. New You. New World.

FUELing Your Life develops the skills that light the path to a fulfilling life experience. That's a lot better than just changing your life. Greater perspectives lead to enhanced life experiences. New view. New you. New world. Of course, a practice without effort is like a car with no tires. The more often I make the effort, the better I get. The better I get, the less effort the practice takes, until it becomes a feel-good experience, and an empowering lifestyle.

I don't have to choose between changing my life, changing my mind, or finding my Soul. I can have all three: enhanced life experiences, updated software, and Conscious expansion. I can enjoy the expansion of my bigger picture physically, mentally and spiritually.

FUEL Your Life is a self-empowerment for every life experience.

FUEL Your Life is a four-point living meditation, woven into the fabric of everyday life. It supports me in accessing an authentic life experience. It's more than just additional self-growth information. These are concepts that anyone can live, anytime, anywhere. FUEL Your Life is a self-empowerment for every life experience. These practices help to build metacognitive skills, or the occurrence of thought recognizing itself. Once thought is able to recognize the programming, it is capable of updating or deleting the programming.

The Epiphany

Spiritual awakening is to experience the epiphany of the separation of thought and Self.

Thought recognizing itself is the prelude to the epiphany. The unlearned, deep-seated knowing spontaneously emerges from inside, that thought is thought, and more importantly, it is not Self. Spiritual awakening is to experience the epiphany of the separation of thought and Self. It is to go beyond the analytical understanding, into the knowing that I am not my identity, but That which witnesses it.

Only in walking sleep, does pain and suffering exist.

As I practice flowing emotion, unconditional acceptance, witnessing thought, and exercising lucidity, I facilitate my own evolution. In turn, I am influencing the evolution of humankind. The objective is to stay awake, for we do indeed sleepwalk. Only in walking sleep, does pain and suffering exist.

FUEL Up

*Self-kindness fuels
the journey back to Self.*

The FUEL Your Life practices demonstrate self-kindness. Self-kindness fuels the journey back to Self. To more easily remember the four points of these practices, I created the acronym, FUEL.

FUEL Your Life
F - **F**low emotion
U - Accept **U**nconditionally
E - Be the **E**yewitness
L - Step into **L**ucidity

FLOW EMOTION

Clear The Runway

An emotion has a natural progression. It begins with a thought. Thoughts, both noticed and unnoticed, create the chemical reactions that create emotion. It's not personal. It's a natural process.

Every emotion that the mind prevents from completing a natural cycle of being felt and released in the moment, results in another unprocessed emotion that I carry around with me. The practice of flowing emotion is meant to give all those pent-up, pushed-away, shunned, and suppressed emotions a chance to be acknowledged, and to fly free.

Each time I witness my emotions, wordlessly embrace them, and watch them dissipate in the moment, I am lightening my load. I am freeing myself. I am taking responsibility for my life experience, and clearing my runway for takeoff.

Don't Shoot The Messenger

Emotions are messengers.

The thought and feeling process is not dependent on the mind deeming a thought true or untrue. We are not spared the bad feelings if we mistake a shadow for a monster. When we believe something that isn't true, or when we are in resistance, feel-bad emotions come to our rescue to wake us up to it. Emotions are messengers.

In unawareness, I mistakenly believe that an emotion is some sort of confirmation of my story or belief. When my mind is totally associated with thought, I believe the unexamined fear that I feel. I'm sleepwalking in a circle. From the mind, to the body, from the body back to the mind. Around I go.

In awareness, I see this unconscious process. I see how unexamined thought creates feel-bad emotion. I recognize the mind immediately trying to reason, deny, or eradicate what feels bad, instead of acknowledging the emotion and letting it flow.

Not noticing unassessed thought as a source of discomfort, and not honoring my emotions, perpetuates fear and suffering, incapacitating me in my life. Positive efforts are counterbalanced by this unconscious habit. I wonder why I can't improve, change or fix things. I can't change what I don't see.

Discomfort is the alarm clock that awakens me to my own misunderstandings and resistance.

I awaken to the message of my discomfort. When I recognize its source, my own misunderstandings and resistance, I am free. Discomfort is the alarm clock that awakens me to my own misunderstandings and resistance.

Surviving Or Thriving

The brain deems uncomfortable or painful emotions as dangerous, and pushes them down or away. You may think that not feeling your emotions is sustaining your survival, but what it is doing is preventing you from thriving. Suppressing your emotions keeps you disconnected from life.

The discomfort of unprocessed emotion, is a warning signal that the waters are rising and the dam is being compromised. Eventually the ignored emotion builds up enough pressure, that back-up may be required to keep it contained. Back-up comes in many forms, such as comfort eating, smoking, drinking alcohol, and other excesses or addictions. No amount of reasoning can make that a good deal.

When opportunity knocks, I don't want to be stuck with an armful of unprocessed emotional baggage. With all that baggage, my choices become governed by the avoidance of the painful emotions, instead of governed by what makes me happy. This is the difference between surviving and thriving. When opportunity knocks, I want to be able to open the door.

The Way Out Is Through

Emotions were meant to be felt and released. They were not meant to be pent up or sustained. Like a boiling teapot, I alleviate the pressure by releasing some of the steam of an emotionally charged issue.

There is a difference between emotions that are perpetuated by the retelling of a story, and emotions that momentarily appear and dissolve in mental silence. The first sustains and prolongs the feel-bad feelings, aggravating the situation. The latter frees me, facilitating the natural flow of emotion, whereby the discomfort begins to fall away.

Contrary to dissociating, diverting, or resisting emotion, I embrace it. I allow emotion the chance to have its say, as opposed to feeding the fire by rehashing a story. I acknowledge the distressing situation from more of a bird's-eye view, as not to fall submersed into the story line. I silently acknowledge and witness emotion as it manifests and evaporates. This has nothing to do with vindication. The mind must temporarily let go of the story, and instead place its quiet attention on feeling, devoid of any mental evaluation.

> *If you try to get past the storm, you will take it with you. The way out, is through.*

A day that I do not take a few moments to silently feel, is a day that I'm not fully going with my own flow of emotion. If you try to get past the storm, you will take it with you. The way out, is through.

Go With The Flow

At first, learning how to affectively feel and flow emotion felt new, and a little scary to me. Patience and self-kindness, coupled with the tenacity to make the effort for myself, made all the difference. This was a skill that I slowly acclimated to. I don't encourage single-handedly taking on monumental pent-up emotion. If you are overwhelmed, please reach out for help.

Flowing emotion is a simple, gentle process, meant to allow what may arise, to come and go freely. There are no stringent rules or set time. Nature is on its own clock. Don't let it become about the steps or the process. The real, however underlying, practice is getting the thinking mind out of the way. Allow what emerges to come and go naturally. This is not a question of capability. It is a question of willingness.

Use Your Tools

Flowing emotion is facilitated by using the other FUEL Your Life practices. Unconditional acceptance of what's happening in the moment allows me to go with the flow, as opposed to stalling out in judgement or resistance.

Being the eyewitness to thought enables me to notice and briefly let go of any thought that may pop up. Staying lucid keeps me out of the story. Falling into the story while flowing emotion adds to my emotional load, increasing and sustaining my discomfort. Staying out of the story while flowing emotion lessens my emotional load, offering the empowerment of healing and freedom.

Wordlessly witness and feel.
That's all there is to do.

I practice witnessing emotion without mentally identifying with it. I watch sensations come and go in a natural, fluid way. Although a story or memory may emerge, allowing emotion to flow is a feeling process, not a thinking process. Wordlessly witness and feel. That's all there is to do.

Grounding

I begin with finding a quiet place to sit undisturbed. Closing my eyes, I quiet the mind the best that I could. I witness thought float by, but don't fall into it. I take a few long, slow, deep breaths.

By placing my wordless attention on my body, breathing, and/or any external stimuli, I am grounding myself in the present moment. If I'm having difficulty focusing, I sometimes place my attention at the top of the head, slowly scanning and relaxing the body, all the way down to the feet.

Opening The Gate

Paying silent mental attention to emotion is the crux of this endeavor.

To flow emotion, I acknowledge the thought, belief or situation at hand. It is a tipping-of-the-hat acknowledgement, not a full reenactment. Flowing emotion does not require me to retell, rehash, or relive a situation. The more thought I associate to, the easier it is for me to fall unconscious into the story, where my efforts then backfire. Paying silent mental attention to emotion is the crux of this endeavor.

I don't even need a particular situation in mind. I can sit quietly and something will come up, or not. Occasionally there is an emotion that's chomping at the bit, wanting so badly to be recognized. It quickly meets my silent invitation. It doesn't need a name or a description. The emotion only needs to be felt, and released.

I sit quietly, as if I were in a theater waiting for a movie to begin. I place my wordless attention on my body. I watch it as an objective eyewitness. I monitor the physical sensations and emotions. I witness them without mental comment.

Letting It Flow And Letting It Go

On occasion I notice that my teeth are clenched, or my muscles are contracted. I may feel anger, sadness, disappointment or fear. I may laugh, and I may spend the next few minutes crying. How the flow of emotion unfolds, has nothing to do with evaluation, opinion or judgement.

I may feel a sudden and slight pinch somewhere, maybe in the neck. I hold my silent attention on it until it moves or changes. I may then feel a slight pressure on the chest. The sensation in the chest could move down to the abdomen, where it may crescendo into a wave of emotional energy.

I lovingly embrace and thoroughly feel the emotion through, without mental identification or rationalization. Wrapping my silent, loving focus around the emotion, it rises up in intensity, and then begins to vanish like smoke.

Placing my focus on the sensations in the body, without a story running in the head, allows the emotion to melt away. I don't have to keep it at bay. I don't have to run from it, or avoid living any part of my life because of it. By surpassing fear and fully feeling the emotion in the moment, I recondition the mind to learn that flowing feel-bad emotion will not destroy me. Flowing emotion frees, heals and empowers me.

We install empowering programing by facing our fears. My inner wiring and my life experience go hand in hand. This is a process to release unneeded, heavy, negative energy. Negative energy created by unnoticed thought.

Fly Free

Almost every time that I thoroughly flow an emotion, it is followed by the reflex response of a wonderful, deep, cleansing breath. Within the exhalation I feel lighter, freer, and empowered. Occasionally I have felt spent afterward. Sometimes, a realization may be experienced, but it is not required. Flowing emotion creates personal rocket fuel. Situations begin to change for the better.

Once you get the gist of flowing emotion, it happens more easily and more often. That's the point, to make a habit of it. The more I do it, the better I feel, the more healing and freedom I experience. Let it become automatic runway clearance, allowing you to become airborne in your own authentic life.

UNCONDITIONAL ACCEPTANCE

Let go or be dragged.
-Zen proverb

What It's Not

The concept of unconditional acceptance is best described by what it is not. Unconditional acceptance does not mean that I condone, or approve something. To fully accept does not mean that I agree with, or even like something. Acceptance does not indicate right or wrong.

Unconditional acceptance frees us
from what hurts, without diminishing
our capacity to love, forgive or heal.

Unconditional acceptance is simply an acknowledgement of the isness of a situation. It is to recognize that something happened, or exists. It is accepting that it already is what it is, in this moment. That's all, no story necessary. It is in resistance to reality that I remain hampered and held back. Unconditional acceptance frees us from what hurts, without diminishing our capacity to love, forgive or heal.

*Acceptance, like love, isn't acceptance
unless it's unconditional.*

Sure it's easy to accept an unexpected check in the mail, or being excluded from your great-aunt's embroidery circle. But it's hard to accept losing your job, or finding your first white hair. Resistance is futile, and a sure-shot recipe for unneeded discomfort. I can't claim that God or the Universe is an omniscient force that does not make mistakes....*except for this one thing right here*. Acceptance, like love, isn't acceptance unless it's unconditional.

Notes From The Universe

I'm continually getting notes from the Universe. Some are sweet little messages, and some seem like nasty hate mail. The way my life speaks to me manifests in many forms, all pointers to my highest good. I would be remiss to take it personally or to resist the messenger.

Being attached to an idea of the way things should be, is one of the greatest sources of pain and derailment. Let's face it, the thinking mind loves trying to contort reality to what it wants it to be. What comes between me and acceptance, is needless thought and resistance. When I accept unconditionally, I allow my own well-being. I'm open to my highest good, in whatever form it may come.

You can fly, when you surrender to the wind.

I'm not suggesting that we throw up our hands, and belly flop into surrender. I can still dream, plan and build. I can do it much better in acceptance. What is, is guidance. I can either read the sign posts of reality and flow with them, or I can resist, and fall out in discomfort and frustration. Unconditional acceptance inherently provides solutions. Let it be easy. You can fly, when you surrender to the wind.

Beyond The Concept

Unconditional acceptance is an experience that is preceded by its conceptual understanding. It is not the conceptual understanding.

The magic of unconditional acceptance lies in experiencing it. Unconditional acceptance is an experience that is preceded by its conceptual understanding. It is not the conceptual understanding. I make sure that I'm not just getting myself to recite some words that make logical sense. That would be empty lip service, which isn't necessarily a bad thing if it makes me feel better. The draw back to lip service is that, at best, its positive affects are temporary.

Making Rocket Fuel Out Of Lemons

To experience unconditional acceptance, I begin by getting lucid, or present outside of unnecessary thought. I acknowledge the situation and wordlessly embrace it. I may not like it or agree with it, and I may want to change it faster than I can blink. That's okay. All I have to do is keep my wordless attention on what I'm feeling.

Most often, I experience unconditional acceptance as a burning sensation in my upper abdomen. It may be accompanied by the countenance of disgust, or even the grinding of teeth. I have felt the flames of resistance lick the back of my throat, as my thinking mind begged me to open my mouth and scorch people where they stood. Rather than explode into a tirade of resistance, I choose to internally embrace the burn. It feels like an internal game of tug-of-war. It is the burning up of resistance.

In flowing with the experience of unconditional acceptance, I create my own rocket fuel.

I hold on in mental silence until the sensation dissolves. This sounds like a big process, but most often it takes place within a matter of seconds. It's almost like quickly passing through some kind of tunnel. I feel the heel-digging resistance going in, and an inexplicable light, expansive feeling on the way out. I feel the discomfort fall away. The more I practice it, the easier and faster it gets. In flowing with the experience of unconditional acceptance, I create my own rocket fuel.

Each time I surrender into unconditional acceptance, something good happens.

Each time I surrender into unconditional acceptance, something good happens. I know that's a big statement, and this has been my experience. Allowing myself to step outside of my comfort zone has yielded unsurpassed growth, and unexpected joy. People, places and situations, change. That's part of the magic of unconditional acceptance, if you allow it. Acceptance opens my door to miracles.

Ready For Takeoff

The universe is always flowing. It's flowing autonomously, one way, toward my highest good. When I accept unconditionally, I allow the universe to flow through me. I join the current of life, instead of swimming against it.

I practice unconditional acceptance on things that usually make me sweat. Like being the only sane driver in the crazy lane, or having to listen to personal cell phone sagas in public. Practice makes powerful programming. I recognize acceptance as an opportunity for growth, rather than an uncomfortable annoyance. I find that the more difficult the experience of acceptance, the bigger the surge of personal rocket fuel.

THE EYEWITNESS

The Big Reveal

According to researchers, including the National Science Foundation, it is estimated that we have between 50,000 and 70,000 thoughts per day. That's roughly 2,000 to 2,900 thoughts per hour, or 35 to 49 thoughts per minute. As remarkable as those numbers seem, I believe that for most of us those numbers are even higher. Maybe not back in the day of little houses on the prairie, but certainly in the day of real-time technology.

We think thoughts, apply reasoning, and formulate beliefs. The problem is that our thoughts and beliefs aren't necessarily true, or in our highest good. How many of the roughly 60,000 thoughts in your day are absolutely true? How many of them are in your best interest? How many are in the best interest of all?

Developing the ability to notice thought, is one of your superpowers.

When I do not notice thought, it controls me. Imagine that, it controls me because I don't notice it. The mind thinks, and I believe it without question, all day long, everyday. Some unmonitored thought has me on top of the world, and some of it has me hiding under the bed. Developing the ability to notice thought, is one of your superpowers.

Becoming The Eyewitness

Becoming the eyewitness is to awaken into the present moment by noticing thought or emotion. This is a natural and spontaneous happening. It is to recognize a thought or emotion as a separate thing, without associating or attaching to it. There's a thought or an emotion, and here I am, the eyewitness.

By witnessing thought, I'm able to determine which thoughts are helpful, and which are flawed patterns. This is not about the act of categorizing. It is a practice to develop innate, metacognitive skills, or thought's ability to notice itself and its own programming.

Updating, or deleting improper programming beings with this one step, this one habit, this one practice. I must begin to develop the skill of witnessing thought. I can't fix a leak if I don't know where it's coming from. Today I will notice my thoughts.

When you witness some of the thoughts that the mind produces, you discover how many of them are automatic, unfounded, fear-based, and serve the mind-made identity. Clearly, the mind has a mind of its own. Its agenda is to perpetuate thinking and upgrade its identity. As the eyewitness, you are able to take notice of this unmonitored tool, that is the thinking mind.

For example, not noticing fear-based thought for what it is, I would automatically believe it, and try to navigate my life around it. If I do notice fear-based thought as it arises, it immediately puts me in a position of choice. Noticing it, gives me options. Options that I did not have before.

I can choose to examine and question thought, flow the thought-produced emotion, accept unconditionally, and/or step completely out of thought into lucidity. All of these options put me in direct access to my own power. That's much better than just believing offhand, fearful thought and suffering the consequences.

Man Overboard

Thought happened, and my mind believed it. I didn't even give myself the chance to examine the thought before I just swallowed it whole. I didn't notice the painful feelings that followed. My alarm clock of feel-bad was ringing, and I didn't notice.

In awareness, I witness thought and allow it to slide on by. In unawareness, the same thoughts turn out to be the open gate that leads me into unconsciousness. The more I am immersed in and focused on the activity in the head, the less available I am to become the eyewitness. This is similar to the captain of a ship being so focused on watching the activity of the rough waters, that he forgets to man his own ship.

Check In

How could we influence possibility? Can we lure the spontaneous happening of becoming the eyewitness? There are ways to tilt the scale in our favor. Try setting an alarm to sound every few hours. It serves as a reminder to silently notice the internal climate of thought and emotion. By repetition, create the habit of checking in with yourself as the eyewitness every time you're at a red light, in an elevator, or on a bathroom break. You could tie a string around your finger, post some wake-up notes, or even schedule a five minute slot for monitoring thought and emotion in your daily planner.

I'd like to think that setting an intention carries the most weight. "Today I intend to become the eyewitness and notice thought and emotion." You will find yourself spontaneously popping awake. You will begin to notice thought and emotion in a new way, recognizing it as something separate from Self. Something that, when left unmonitored, is the source of discomfort.

Downtempo

Sometimes it feels like I can barely keep up with my to-do list, much less monitor my rapid-firing thoughts. I've learned that slowing myself down really helped. I mean specifically, taking myself down a notch in the moment. I take a deep breath, come into the present moment, and slow down my thoughts, speech, and physical movement, even if it's just a bit.

Sure enough, this helps me to catch more of the thoughts gallivanting through my head. I notice thoughts that the mind really has no way of knowing are absolutely true. When I slow down and pay attention to what I'm thinking or saying, I discover untruths and resistance that would have otherwise run amok.

Purge-Journaling

Purge-journaling is my way of exposing additional painful thoughts and beliefs. Allowing my thinking mind a short, quick rant, to say whatever it feels in the moment, always turns out to be telling. Afterward I read what I journaled as the unbiased eyewitness, and spot the thoughts and beliefs that are packed with a negative punch. I learned that the thoughts that hurt the most were the ones that needed my attention, not my resistance.

Purge-journaling also made it a lot easier to zoom out of the story, and get a bird's-eye view of the situation. This is an advantageous perspective. It supports me in being able to view the situation in an objective way.

What Else Is True?

If a thought feels bad, I am either believing an untruth, or I am in resistance to something. This is the source of all pain and suffering.

If a thought feels good, great. If a thought feels bad, I am either believing an untruth, or I am in resistance to something. This is the source of all pain and suffering. While it may be helpful to determine the answers to some of the mind's questions, getting lost in asking them ushers me into unconsciousness and discomfort. Once I notice a feel-bad thought, all I have to do is to remember that there is a realization to be had.

A realization reveals Truth, and washes away my discomfort. Truth comes from higher intelligence, which is outside of thought. When I quiet the mind, I invite truth to emerge. There are only two places to stand. I am either tethered to thought, or I am free.

If I can't see reality outside of the mind's interpretation of it, I'm not seeing the bigger picture.

The truth is always there, and does go unrecognized. If I can't see reality outside of the mind's interpretation of it, I'm not seeing the bigger picture. Looking at life through the confines of the mind's learned beliefs, is like taking something out of context, reading only one sentence of a story, or focusing on only one piece of a larger puzzle. I look at a feel-bad situation and ask myself, "What else is true?" Finding what else is also true about a person or situation, enables me to see through what feels bad, and to experience freedom, growth, healing, and peace.

As the eyewitness, from a bird's-eye view, I can easily see what else is true.

I look to myself. In awareness, I step into vulnerability. I remind myself that no thought, story, or belief is certain, and that everything supports my awakening. I look inside of myself with honesty, and a willingness to find truth. I am willing to be wrong. I am willing to see things in a different way. I am willing to discover what the mind is overlooking. As the eyewitness, from a bird's-eye view, I can easily see what else is true.

See, Not Say

As the eyewitness, I take my real, honest thought or belief, and sit with it until I see my misunderstanding and/or resistance. My freedom lies in seeing through the thought or belief, back to myself. It is not about applying a new story to the thought or belief. Realization is a falling away of unawareness. It is the rising of Truth. It is a visceral experience that feels expansive, and like the dropping of a heavy load. It is an innate knowing, versus a belief in a new story. In other words, you suddenly recognize something you did not see before.

> *First there is the intellectual understanding.*
> *Beyond that is instinctual knowing.*

I don't make this distinction to imply that you must have an earth-shattering realization to experience positive change. That's not the case. Mental reasoning alone can bring us to new perspectives that benefit all. This is how to begin. These mental efforts, these new practices, beckon the experience of unprompted realization. First, there is the intellectual understanding. Beyond that is instinctual knowing. Love and appreciate yourself for the courage to make the effort that gets you there.

Now Or Then

Time is irrelevant. I am able to find my truths by witnessing thoughts and stories from both the past and present. For instance, years ago I had a difficult situation at work. I was shocked to discover an associate secretly and purposefully sabotaging my workflow. I had always looked back on this situation with uneasiness, until I was able to see the bigger picture.

After acknowledging this memory, I sat quietly and asked myself, *What else is true?* As the impartial eyewitness, I opened myself up to seeing what I was missing. I did not formulate thoughts of what else could be true from supposition or assumption. Like an outfielder, I silently waited for something to fall into my hands. As each honest observation and realization flew in, I caught them without opinion:

-This associate was acting out of fear. Fear of not having her presentation completed by the same deadlines that we all faced.
-I assumed all components of my work were going as planned, and I assumed wrong.

-She taught me that it is in my best interest to check on the progress of my projects, while they are in the hands of others.
-She taught me that she sabotages.
-This situation was an opportunity for me to step up for myself, in a professional and peaceful way, with self-confidence and self-appreciation.
-This experience opened my eyes to things that I didn't see before, and to my own naivete.
-I learned beneficial new practices, which I added to my arsenal of good management skills.

As the eyewitness, I recognized that we all get scared. That doesn't make this woman's behavior right. It does not mean that I have to go back for more. Seeing this situation as the unbiased eyewitness, endowed me with effectual realization, that benefited me even beyond the workplace. So while this person was indeed secretly and purposefully sabotaging my workflow, it was also true that her actions offered me self-growth and empowerments. Becoming the eyewitness moves me into my circle of awareness, where I may trade discomfort for freedom and growth.

LUCIDITY

Awake In The Dream

There are two states of being. If I don't see that, I don't see lucidity. To be lucid is to be present in the moment, outside of unnecessary thought. It is to perceive life without narration. From this space I'm able to acknowledge thought if it pops up, without falling unconscious into a story. It's very much like being the eyewitness, but with an extra layer of awareness.

Lucidity is gaining
Consciousness in the dream.

Lucidity is prefaced with the ah-ha moment of distinguishing between Consciousness and unconsciousness. It is self recognizing Self. Lucidity is gaining Consciousness in the dream.

Say What?

Let's say you told me that when you fall asleep, your dream turns into a nightmare, and you don't know what to do about it. I tell you that the solution is simple. Every time you fall asleep and a nightmare begins, just wake yourself up.

You'd probably tell me how ridiculous that suggestion is. After all, if you were easily able to wake yourself up from a nightmare, you wouldn't have a problem. This is the human condition. I am pointing at waking up, when we fall unconscious into our own waking nightmares. To be lucid is to be awake.

On Or Off?

In lucidity I am free to experience life firsthand, without the filter of my history or habitual behavior.

When I'm off, I am submersed in and identified with thoughts and stories. I am reacting to life from assimilated behavior, saying and doing the same things in the same ways. When I'm on, I'm lucid. In lucidity I am free to experience life firsthand, without the filter of my history or habitual behavior. I can offer life my full attention, and in return experience the rush of a direct connection.

I practice being present with my own awareness. I practice keeping a quiet mind, while being aware of the inner mood of thought and emotion. I silently witness, monitor or hover awareness, around thoughts and feelings. No story, no words, just witnessing. This is similar to a parent or guardian monitoring their children while performing other tasks.

At first, lucidity may feel like a mental juggling act. With patience and practice, it gets easier. Eventually the disparity between being lucid and being enveloped in thought is apparent, and lucidity quickly becomes the preferred state. Ultimately, I experience life with less of the mental analysis, inner labeling, judging, and evaluating. I am directly connected to life, thinking about it less, and experiencing it more.

Turn Yourself On

Think of lucidity like a lamp. A lamp that you could turn on just by paying attention to it. As long as you hold some of your attention on the lamp, the light stays on. When your light is on, you see life clearly. The minute your attention becomes completely submersed in thought or outside activity, your light goes out and you find yourself "in the dark." Gently bringing my attention back to the present moment wakes me up. When my light is on, I can tell the difference between a monster and a shadow. That changes everything.

What's A Thinking Mind To Do?

When an adverse story rises up, I recognize it as unproductive thinking. I either replace it with positive thought, or I step outside of the mental speculation, into the silent awareness of lucidity.

Sometimes I feel as if my focus needs to be fixed on something, to prevent falling back into a story. Zooming in on the sights, smells, sounds and sensations of the present moment are excellent anchors in lucidity. Even if I'm in a quiet, desolate place, I can always focus on breathing. I can do these things at home, in a meeting, or waiting on line in the supermarket.

That's the easy part. The hard part is dismissing the pull of the thinking mind. Those fear-based thoughts that call out, swelling with angst, to get us to abandon our peace, and jump back into an inner dialog. Every time I resist tumbling back into gratuitous thought, my efforts are lending themselves to the breaking of a bad habit. I am chipping away at old programming that is not in my best interest, and reprogramming with innate, life changing skills.

Lucidity is not a measuring stick, nor is it meant to be another feather stuck in the cap of the self-made identity. This practice is meant to be done in the same way that I am meant to enjoy my life, moment by moment. When I recognize my own unconsciousness, I stop and bring myself back to me, back to my silent Self.

Feel-Good Solutions

Wield your powers for good.

It is advantageous to reinforce the life-changing practice of lucidity, by acknowledging the fruitful efforts of the thinking mind. This kind of momentary, positive reinforcement is the seed to the sprouting of self-reliance and self-appreciation. We have the power to wire feel-good to our endeavors. Wield your powers for good.

Lucidity is a living meditation.

By maintaining lucidity, I give myself a well deserved break from the incessant mental chatter. This reduces mental, emotional and physical stress. It gives me a moment to recharge. Lucidity is a living meditation.

Intuition trumps reasoning.

When I step outside of surplus thought that is nonessential to my survival, I cut down on the inner static, and am better able to hear and/or feel Guidance. I open the space for opportunity, and novel ideas to surface. I beckon the muse, and open the door to intuition. Reasoning guesses, intuition knows. Intuition trumps reasoning.

When the thinking mind concedes to Self, it accesses potential it did not have before.

I am not suggesting that you should never think things through. Should you feel comfortable thinking something through, go right ahead. You may also consider dedicating a few moments of lucidity to the situation, to see if any realizations or ideas pop up that you hadn't thought of. When the thinking mind concedes to Self, it accesses potential it did not have before. It is then capable of things it has not done before. You have a connection to higher intelligence. You may as well use it.

The Gold Ring

Gaining lucidity is a spontaneous happening. Like spotting the golden ring while riding the merry-go-round. It's maintaining lucidity that is the practice. I earnestly intend to notice thought, and with that, awaken into the separation of Consciousness (Self) and unconsciousness (thought).

The Dance Of Awakening

-I gain lucidity.
-I unwittingly fall back into unconsciousness, submersed in thought.

-I gain lucidity.
-I unwittingly fall back into unconsciousness, submersed in thought.

-Step in, step out. I am dancing the dance of awakening.

PRACTICING THE PRACTICE

Flowing In The Right Direction

The four points of FUEL Your Life can be practiced separately or together, and in any order. They are meant to be used as needed, in the moment. The practice is always simple, but it is not always easy. When I experience freedom that only a realization can offer, I know I'm walking in the right direction.

These practices are meant to take on a rhythm of their own. They are your tools. FUELing your life is a lifestyle. It is an unlearning and a relearning. It is a deprogramming and reprogramming. It invites and supports authentic change, healing, growth, and freedom.

How Can I Help, How Can I Serve?

My thinking mind's primary purpose is to assist my higher Self. To do this, I make an effort to FUEL my life. I allow emotion to flow, and I strive to accept unconditionally. I practice witnessing thought and emotion, questioning them when needed. I exercise lucidity, perceiving life with a quiet mind.

*Authentic living is a life lived in pleasure,
not a life lived in the avoidance of pain.*

With each small effort, I add to my own empowerment. Practicing these perspectives in my everyday life, escorts me into the easy and effortless flow of authenticity. Authentic living is a life lived in pleasure, not a life lived in the avoidance of pain.

We do what's familiar. We don't realize that we're living within the confines of unquestioned thought and repeated reactions. Living inside of a comfort zone of rote thinking and behavior, keeps us from having the life that we really want to live. We spend our lives exerting effort after effort, and wondering why nothing moves. It's time to step out of old behavior and into the life you came here for.

Keeping Your Balls In The Air

To get familiar with the FUEL Your Life perspectives, practice each of them, one at a time. Dedicate a few days or a full week, to focus on and live each perspective separately. Continue this living meditation in your daily life, calling on any one of the four perspectives as needed. Eventually, you will notice that you naturally begin to combine these perspectives, practicing them in unison.

These practices are driven by the impetus of our focus. It is for that reason, that practicing them in combination feels similar to juggling. We're sharing our attention between acceptance and lucidity, while monitoring thought and emotion. We're juggling. Ultimately, you'll have all four balls in the air.

This feels similar to learning to dance or to drive a car. At first it may feel a bit daunting, but before long you're rolling along effortlessly. Practicing the FUEL Your Life perspectives awakens our innate abilities. We are naturally equipped to thrive in an awakened, authentic life experience.

All Bliss, No Blister

Wait, there's more. After test driving each practice, and then living them in combination, the inexplicable ignites. All four efforts meld into one blissful state of being. That means that all my balls are in the air, on autopilot. All bliss, no blister. Nirvana.

Presence: Having all of your balls in the air.

I have experienced this state intermittently. The shift happens unannounced and spontaneously. I am the lucid eyewitness, flowing emotion in mental silence and unconditional acceptance. The low and steady buzz of excitement feeds the awe. It is a state where that just being, is fulfilling and glorious. This exquisite state comes and goes to varying degrees. This is the blissful state of Presence. Presence: having all of your balls in the air.

The Fab Four

The beauty of this power-packed quartet is that I could employ any one of these practices in whatever order, combination, or frequency that I'm most comfortable with. In other words, I don't figure it out as much as I feel it out, and go with the flow. These are my tools and they are at my disposal. The real power lies in exercising these tools in my everyday life, no matter how, when or where I do it.

FUEL Your Life

F - **F**low emotion
Today I will live my life from the inside out.

U - Accept **U**nconditionally
Today I will make reality my friend and teacher.

E - Be the **E**yewitness
Today I will be the eyewitness to thought, so that I may discard those that do not serve.

L - Step into **L**ucidity
Today I will practice lucidity, so that I may connect to Guidance, Intuition and Life itself.

EMPOWERMENT:
I have come fully equipped for this adventure. Today I intend to FUEL my life.

PART THREE

FIFTY SHADES
OF AWAKENING

We did not come only to awaken from this dream.
We came with the ability to awaken IN this dream.
    -Gina Charles, Shift Happens

The fifty shades listed here represent fifty life situations or experiences. These experiences are looked at through the perspectives of FUEL Your Life. It is with hope that pointing toward a realization, facilitates its discovery.

Each shade inherently has two possibilities. I either believe the experience, or I recognize it as an illusion. The more truthful I am willing to be with myself, the greater my realization, freedom, and joy.

ADDICTION

The Symptom

According to definition, addiction is a dependency on something that one is unable to stop without adverse effects. If you are experiencing addiction, you may consider reaching out for help. Not only may your life depend on it, but the quality of your life depends on it.

Albeit destructive, my addiction is a symptom.

Along with the more common addictions, like smoking, drinking, and binge eating, there are a multitude of diverse addictive behaviors. Some people are even addicted to thinking. Regardless of the nature of one's addiction, the commonality stays the same. Albeit destructive, my addiction is a symptom.

A Call For Back-up

Addiction was born out of my mind's call for back-up. I have a painful thought, and before my brain can even translate it into hormones, the mind almost concurrently executes a resistant response. When it becomes difficult for my thinking mind to maintain its resistance to something, it reaches outside of itself, repeatedly. This conditioned behavior becomes the monster called addiction.

As the eyewitness, I discerned that the feeling of overwhelm prompted me to eat when I wasn't hungry. When in the grips of this triggered reaction, I noticed that my mouth began to salivate. My body had learned the routine, and was responding before I could even get something into my mouth. Pavlov's dogs have got nothing on me.

From The Inside Out

When I quit smoking, I did it from the inside out. I believed that I enjoyed smoking so much, that the only way that I could ever stop, would be if I changed the way I felt about it. How do you get yourself to loathe something you really like? Something you've been doing everyday, for many years? I felt resistance in the thought that quitting may be a long, slow process. Patience wasn't one of my virtues. The only consolation would be to find a gentle procedure.

Past experience led me to believe that will power and discipline would only take me so far. I needed something that would work, but in a gentle enough way that I could live my daily life without trying to scratch someone's eyes out. I wasn't looking for more suffering, I wanted less. I wanted a livable, doable way out, that would provide real and lasting change. For me, baby steps made the difference between getting there and not. While my mind's self-made schedule abhors baby steps, they turned out to be the catalyst of authentic change.

I made lists, just to get myself warmed up to the idea of quitting. I made an honest list of all the bad things about smoking. I made another list of all the benefits of being smoke-free. I paid attention to how each made me feel. Those lists took the form of two powerful visuals, which came in very handy.

One of the visuals was a mental snapshot of how great I'd look and feel 20 smoke-free years from now. The other mental snapshot was how horrifying I'd look and feel 20 smoke-filled years from now. These are the stories I *want* my mind to feel and believe. Everyday, ideally when craving a cigarette, I'd close my eyes, and take a mental look at both of the images in my head. Afterward, if I wanted a cigarette that bad, I'd smoke, even if it were a half of a cigarette.

Reminding myself what an impediment smoking had become was a powerful influence. My mind hates anything that it believes curtails its freedom. I took that and ran with it. Another helpful effort was to keep a notebook with daily recordings of every cigarette smoked, by simply listing the time I smoked it. Over the course of about 8 weeks, the notebook reflected a consistent decline in cigarettes smoked. In addition, I celebrated my willingness to look directly at the bad programming. An occasional pat on the back goes a long way.

I worked on eradicating the seed of the behavior. Instead of suppressing uncomfortable emotion, I did my best to get out of the way of its natural flow. Of course, acceptance of where I was in the moment, assisted me in moving forward. I worked at staying lucid, and aware of my state of being. Being the eyewitness to thought and emotion allowed me to notice the old programming, prompting me to reach outside of myself to the object of my addiction.

Eventually, I had my last half cigarette. The most interesting aspect of this endeavor is that living smoke-free has had nothing to do with will power. I have never craved a cigarette after quitting. With awareness, and patient self-kindness, changing my programming resulted in authentic change. I went from loving to loathing.

Gems In A Basket

When my son was a boy, and throughout his life, I've reiterated my story about *Gems In A Basket*. However cheesy, the concept serves us well. Eventually I realized that this metaphor is really about baby steps.

Every time you learn something empowering, you add a gem to your basket. Every time you grow, do a good deed, follow your own heart, or make any kind of effort toward your highest good, you chuck another gem in your basket. Eventually, the day may come that you need to draw on your own greatness. After years of investing gems in your basket, you will find yourself rich beyond your wildest dreams.

Each time I craved a cigarette, and paused in lucidly to notice and interrupt the pull of addiction, I added a gem to my basket. Yes, even if I had smoked a cigarette afterward. Each time I was able to dismiss negative thought just by noticing it, I gained another gem. Every time I made the effort to keep track of how much I was smoking, I added another gem to my basket. Each time I mentally compared the mental images of being smoke-free to being smoke-filled, and flowed those emotions, I invested gems in my basket.

Every little thing I did differently, especially when the trigger to have a cigarette was firing in my brain, eventually and collectively, changed my programming. Ultimately, I had enough gems in my basket, and was ready and able to successfully walk away. To this day if I smell a cigarette, I experience a tremendous distaste for it.

Breaking Free

The best time to strike is when the iron is hot. Noticing the pull of addictive behavior is the magic moment. As the eyewitness, I catch those magic moments. It is my opportunity to weaken the pull of that behavior by responding differently than what the behavior is telling me to do, even for just a few moments. Whatever I do that is different from the programmed behavior, is helping to change my life. Every effort, no matter how small, counts. With each little effort, I create another chip in the wall, until I break through, and experience the freedom of authentic change.

You have to get real with yourself. It's not about beating yourself up. That's unconsciousness. Getting real about the isness of things is empowering. Get so real that the moment becomes surreal. This is the moment of truth. You're standing on the threshold of realization. You're standing on the threshold of your own power and freedom.

Addiction is not what I am, it's bad programming.

Unconditional acceptance of an addiction frees me to change my situation. Addiction is not what I am, it's bad programming. Allowing emotion to come and go in a natural flow, helps to disengage its pull. Practicing lucidity is a rewiring, that keeps me out of the old, painful, fallacious thinking. I choose to live in the space of boundless potential, instead of trapped in a life of avoidance. I found my tools, and I'm going to use them.

EMPOWERMENT:
With each *gem in my basket*, I'm changing my programming, and my life experience. Baby steps get me there.

ANGER

The Short Strings

Anger = nonacceptance.

Anger is a spitfire emotion. It can manifest itself as a raised eyebrow, or internalized rolling thunder. Whether it's an occasional upset, or anger that lands you behind bars, it's all a feel-bad experience. Anger really wants my attention. It has an urgent message for me. Anger is alerting me that I have become engulfed in a story that says something is wrong with what is. Our stories are so powerful that we become fully engaged with them. If I believe that there is something wrong with the reality of this moment, I am having a misunderstanding. Anger = nonacceptance.

It is the unexamined thinking that angers me,
and it is the unexamined thinking that controls me.

Anger is disempowering. If I find myself easily angered on a daily basis, I have cultivated the habit of anger, and am now a puppet on the short strings of bad programming. It is the unexamined thinking that angers me, and it is the unexamined thinking that controls me.

Set It Free

There's a big difference between flowing the emotion of anger, and being angry. Flowing the emotion of anger is releasing the emotion. Being angry is reinforcing the bars in which anger has me held captive.

To flow the emotion of anger, I apply my silent mental focus to the internal feelings that arise. Evaluations, explanations, and reasoning impede the natural flow of emotion. Quite often, other emotions surface. Hurt hides behind anger. I cradle the sensations and emotions in as much mental silence as I can muster, until they peak and release. All flow, no story.

Practice Makes Programming

Retelling the story from the anger of your original perspective is reinforcing the problem.

We rant, venting an angry story, in an attempt at feeling better. Until I am willing to tell the story from an honest place, and willing to see what is, rather than where I think I'm right, then it's not worth reiterating. Retelling the story from the anger of your original perspective is reinforcing the problem.

Repeatedly revisiting anger has a cumulative and detrimental affect. While reliving anger, my thinking mind is practicing what feeling bad feels like. Practice makes programming.

If I found myself retelling the same anger-filled stories, maybe I'm feeding a story of victimization, or helplessness. No matter how I slice anger, retelling, reliving, ranting, repeating, or regurgitating it, only keeps me hurting, unconscious, and disempowered.

Do I want to be angry, or do I want to be free?

The choice is always mine. Do I want to be angry, or do I want to be free? Am I willing to be honest with myself in the name of my own freedom, healing and happiness? Do I love myself enough to look for my truth, instead of for the empty label of being wronged?

Moving Forward

There are those occasions where letting out a bit of steam feels like it could do a body good. Take a jog, work out, scream obscenities into a pillow, or lift the couch up over your head a few times. But for goodness sake, don't fall back into the story. Releasing a bit of angry energy often facilitates moving on to the wordless flow of emotion.

Once I take that sharp edge off of anger, I'm free to practice unconditional acceptance of what is. I certainly do not have to like it, I just have to acknowledge that it already is. Unconditional acceptance eliminates resistance. When I eliminate resistance, I see things that I did not notice before. I see what else is also true about a person or situation. I see my anger in context, and clarity emerges. In clarity, I transform my life.

EMPOWERMENT:
I free and empower myself by responding to anger in lucidity, rather than reacting to anger in unconsciousness.

ANXIETY

The Call

Negative thought is food for anxiety.

When you are experiencing anxiety, you really don't care how you got there, you just want out. This holds true for pangs of uneasiness, to outright, full-blown panic attacks. No matter what the degree, anxiety is the painful result of repeated episodes of negativity. Negative thought is food for anxiety.

Anxiety is the previously unanswered
wake-up call for unconsciousness.

I have painful thoughts, and I believe them. I tell painful stories, endure the bad feelings that follow, and continue to repeat it all, to myself and others. Then I wonder why life sometimes seems too painful to bear, as if life were causing it. Anxiety is the previously unanswered wake-up call for unconsciousness.

Five-Alarm Fire

When my insides started ringing like the bells of a five-alarm fire, I didn't know what was happening. That strong, engulfing feeling of anxiety rose up like a life-threatening wave, sweeping me away from the inside. The first time I experienced this, it took my breath away, literally. I did not see it coming. I had no idea that I had been disregarding my inner promptings, long enough for the Universe to send me a message that it knew I couldn't ignore.

Anxiety. This is my brain on stories.

I now see that it was all on me. I had cultivated the habit of believing feel-bad thoughts without noticing them. I made a practice of maintaining the negative feelings that were perpetuated by superfluous thought and storytelling. Unobserved thought gains enough momentum to smack you down, when thinking is not balanced with being. Anxiety. This is my brain on stories.

Where There's Smoke There's Fire

I had to muster up some super-sized courage to accept the isness of an anxiety-filled moment. Each second that I made the effort to accept what was happening, the more the anxiety disappeared. I was also teaching or programming the thinking mind that accepting a moment such as this will not kill me. Unconditional acceptance was the door marked "Exit."

Having stepped up to this experience in the throes of anxiety, however brief it may have been, made it much easier to practice acceptance in my daily life. After all, what's the use of clearing the smoke without putting out the fire?

The little fires in my life occur when I do not allow the flow of emotion, when I do not accept, and when I am submersed in unmonitored thought. Keeping out the fire of nonacceptance, being the eyewitness to thought, flowing emotion, and practicing lucidity, has kept anxiety at bay.

EMPOWERMENT:
Anxiety is the internal roar of unconsciousness. I witness, accept, flow and awaken.

ATTACHMENT

A Fear-Based Story

Attachment is living in fear of loss.

Attachment seemed as if it were this real thing. A first, the idea of it gave me a warm and fuzzy feeling inside. It also filled me with fear, the fear of one day not having the object of my desire. Attachment is living in fear of loss.

Attachment requires a fear-based story.

Don't confuse attachment with love. Unconditional love is part of the flow of life. Love does not depend on being attached to someone or something. Unconditional love requires no story, and comes from Consciousness. Attachment requires a fear-based story. A fear-based story comes from unconsciousness.

Believing Is Feeling

Attachment is born out of a story, or an identity that I assign to someone or something. There's a big difference between *a* bird, and Fred, *my* bird. The more of Fred's identity that corresponds to mine, the stronger my mind's attachment to him.

Feeling attached is a misbelief that says that if I no longer have you, I will lose part of myself, and my happiness. Of course, that's not accurate. You are sitting across from me, and I love you. You are no longer sitting across from me, and I love you. What's the difference between the happiness I had with my beloved, and the pain that I have without my beloved? My focus, my story, and my submersion in it. When sleepwalking, or living bound within the bubble of unperceived thought, the mind believes what it thinks without appraising it. We believe, without considering validity.

Direct Connection

I may very well love with all of my heart. I either love with the pernicious influence of attachment, or without it. Removing the story of attachment allows me to have a direct, authentic connection with the people and things in my life. This produces a fulfilling experience, without the unnecessary pain. Everything changes. Nothing stays the same or stands still. Therein lies the flow of our lives. Outside of attachment we enjoy the flow of the moment. Our lucid experience is devoid of underlying fears and insecurities.

Hold The Sprinkles

*Sprinkling attachment onto the things in
my life only puts me in service to them.*

If I sprinkle a little attachment on my relationships, it begins to govern the relationship. What I do and say thereafter, will be tainted with the fear of loss. Sprinkling attachment onto the things in my life only puts me in service to them.

As the eyewitness, I notice unneeded, fear-based thought that feeds the story of attachment. I recognize attachment as a filter that comes between me and who or what I love. I choose to focus on what feels good, rather than focus on an unnecessary story of loss.

I give fully of myself, knowing that I can never lose what's most important. It is in love and appreciation that I enjoy the people and the things in my life. I can never lose that. It is within me, eternally.

EMPOWERMENT:
Outside of the fear that is attachment, lies a direct and authentic connection of love and enjoyment.

BULLYING

Dig Here

It's hard to see ourselves from someone else's point of view. If you are a bully, I will let you in on something. From the outside, bullying speaks louder than any meritorious attribute. It tells the world that you feel angry, small, and fearful. Bullying is a public display of trying to get yourself to believe that you are bigger, better, stronger, than you really think you are, through the eyes of others.

> ***Bullying is like getting up on your soapbox and announcing to the world how little you really think of yourself.***

Other's are not thinking how great you are. They are either feeling sorry for you, or are secretly thanking you for letting them know you are someone to avoid. Bullying is like getting up on your soapbox and announcing to the world how little you really think of yourself. If you are a bit of a bully and this description really ticks you off, that's a good thing. That's a sign post that says *Dig Here*.

All Gain, No Pain

If you have been bullied, and are still carrying around the pain, please know that you can dump it. Stifled emotions, like sadness, anger or hurt, create burdensome baggage. The mind thinks it's doing us a favor by ignoring uncomfortable emotion, but in actuality it is creating more difficulty.

Carrying around unprocessed emotion is like going through life with a big splinter. Whenever something brushes up against these repressed emotions, it hurts. We invest our energy evading what hurts, rather than investing that energy to eliminate our pain. The pain will continue to point out the splinter, in hopes that we will remove it.

I'm much more willing to feel any emotion, now that I realize that the alternative is to carry it around with me, and to continue to feel the pain. I begin by mentally acknowledging an incident in which I felt bullied, making sure that I don't get lost in the story. Silently, I witness the emotions that swell, while simultaneously letting thought float by like a leaf in the wind. The emotions peak, and then begin to fade away. When I release the painful emotions of being bullied, I'm free.

Pillow Talk Or Poison

How do you talk to yourself? How do you talk to others? Ever notice? Are you supportive and self-loving, or are you depressive and self-deprecating? Whether or not you are aware of how you talk to yourself, or others, today is the day to practice the skill of being the eyewitness to thought.

Find The Bull In Bully

I realize that I had bullied myself in ways that went unrecognized. There were plenty of times where I pushed myself too hard and for too long. Many times that I called myself names, deprived myself, or told myself that I wasn't good enough. I also realize that there were times that I unwittingly bullied others as well.

Self-love finds the bull in bully.

When we don't witness our own thinking, and instead just have and believe it, we don't realize how unconscious and hurtful thought can be. Had I not noticed my bullying thoughts, I would still be meeting the unpleasant experiences that they manifested into my life. I choose to do things differently now. Self-love finds the bull in bully.

EMPOWERMENT:
In awareness, I recognize the unconsciousness of a bully. Self-kindness frees me from bullying self, and bullying others.

CHANGE

Changing My World

In order for me to grow, or to free myself from painful misinterpretations, I must look inward. Understanding that the controls to this ride are on the inside, is the difference between temporary and permanent change.

Our thoughts and beliefs create emotions, and overall feelings or moods. The energy of those feelings are projected outward into the ethers, summoning various life experiences. It's similar to a reflection in a mirror. Why is it like this? To give us the opportunity to see where we can grow and free ourselves from indiscriminate thought. It's a fail-safe of sorts, from unconsciousness. With this mirror concept in mind, I see what a futile attempt it is to reach outside of myself to make any changes in my life.

When stuff changes on the inside, stuff changes on the outside. What is the stuff that changes on the inside? It is my mind. What changes are my thoughts, perspectives and ultimately my programming. My thoughts and beliefs are the filters through which I have this human experience. Changing my mind, changes my world.

Effort Or Enlightenment

Change happens in two ways. One way that change occurs is to execute a plan or technique, with consistent, steadfast effort behind it. The effort is sustained by some form of discipline or will power. Therein lies conditional change, dependent on the longevity and consistency of my efforts.

The other way that change occurs is by waking up. When I see through my thoughts and beliefs, to the actual isness of a situation, the clarity changes my whole experience. The newfound clarity affords me a new perspective, also known as an ah-ha moment or realization. Realization paves the way for authentic change.

Finding My Pearl

There is change that we want, and there is change that we do not want. Of course the more resistance that I exercise, the more difficult and uncomfortable the situation becomes. That's not to say that I shouldn't act. If I respond to change in anger or fear, I worsen my experience. This is my invitation to take another shot at unconditional acceptance. I may not like what's going on, but I am able to accept that it exists.

> *When I act out of inspiration rather than resistance, the situation transforms itself.*

Once I'm able to accept the isness of the moment, no matter how much I'd rather stuff a sock in it, I empower myself. When I act out of inspiration rather than resistance, the situation transforms itself. I know I'm acting out of inspiration when I experience delivering my truths, with no malice or bad feelings on my part. Once I find that pearl in the bag of poop, I no longer need the bag of poop. I then recognize change working in my favor. If I don't get the gift of the lesson, I'm bound to repeat it until I do. Imagine how empowering it is to make friends with change.

Change It

Lucidity and unconditional acceptance keep me gliding in my stride. As the eyewitness I recognize and discard thoughts and beliefs that have me idling in neutral. I may practice stepping out of thought completely. In addition, I honor any emotion that comes up, allowing it to run its course.

Authentic change is also derived by doing the thing we cannot do. You may discover that change is not only about doing what it takes to achieve a goal. It's not all about creating that relationship, or attaining outward success. It may not even be about healing. You may discover that the thing that creates the most positive change in your life, the thing that you could not do, is to be good to yourself. Now you can get to work.

Change is the only constant. Adapting to change serves my highest good, and my evolution. There is always something good in it for me, even if I can't see it from where I'm standing. Changing the world, begins with changing my world. Changing my world, begins within me.

EMPOWERMENT:
I flow with the current of life. I accept and rejoice in opening the gifts of change.

CREATIVITY

The Sacred Space

As an artist, I am familiar with the sacred space of creativity. Authentic creativity is inspirational. It courses through me, manifesting itself through my endeavor. Artists know this as the space in which their best work is done. The experience is wonderfully inexplicable.

The flow of creativity is the space where the brush knows the way. It is the experience of words flowing effortlessly onto a page, or music singing through you. Things fall into place, perfectly. To be in the flow of creativity, is to experience Consciousness bearing itself easily and effortlessly as art, a great idea, a solution, or realization.

I am easily able to identify which of my sketches were done in the flow of creativity, and which were created from the purposeful effort of the mind. The work produced from the flow of creativity has a vibe. It drips with it's own fluidity and unspoken communication. The work produced cerebrally, at best can be savvy, interesting, even beautiful in some way, but it lacks a life of its own. It lacks that ability to silently speak loud and clear.

What Happened?

***Thought, beliefs and resistance
impede the creative flow.***

The muse, just like truth, is always hovering around, tickling us right under our noses. Why don't I recognize it? Thought, beliefs and resistance impede the creative flow. Somewhere along the line, I fell out of the flow of things. I fell into thought. *What if I don't make my deadline? How can my work be bigger or better than the next guy's? I don't have what I need to make this happen. What if they don't like this?*

I insidiously moved my focus out of my gut and into my head. I began looking at the work from the outside, evaluating, judging, labeling, and figuring things out, all in the name of doing good work. Fear-based thought began making my decisions. It only takes one rancid ingredient to ruin the soup.

I pushed myself further, faster, and harder. That only made me angrier, more tired and overwhelmed. All of a sudden, I didn't like the project anymore. I had wired feeling bad to the project, and didn't realize it. Then I wondered what happened. How did I go from enjoying this so much, to hating it?

There's nothing wrong with the left side of my brain chiming in on a creative endeavor. Done ideally, thought is an invaluable tool. It turns ugly when thought is not balanced or outweighed by right-brain lucidity.

Inviting The Muse

What inspires or excites you? If you're decorating a room, look at photos of rooms that make you feel those little sparks of excitement inside. Put yourself in a place, mentally or physically, that feels good. Then move into your other circle, the state of awareness.

*Mental chaos, and fearful
conjecture keep the muse at bay.*

No matter what you're trying to do, the flow of creativity squeezes the juice of authenticity into your endeavor. I am available to the creative flow when I am lucid. Being present in the moment without the surplus cerebral chitchat, better enables me to feel my way through, and into that flow. Mental chaos, and fearful conjecture keep the muse at bay.

Flowing in acceptance and lucidity, I recognize inspiration whispering in my ear, and I follow it blindly. The magic carpet ride begins. It is at this point that I am no longer trying to create something, as much as I am witnessing the project become something. My wordless attention is on the invisible scale in my gut. Feeling my way through, outside of the mental assessment, is the short-cut to the playground of creativity.

EMPOWERMENT:
Feel your way through. The muse lives in lucidity.

CONTROL

Under Control

Control is the thinking mind's ardent desire. The belief in control is the mind's antidote to fear. We believe the ability to control our lives puts us in a position of security, safety, and power, whereby we can avoid pain and suffering.

When I am fully engaged with unmonitored thought, my life is controlled by it.

Today, we have more choices in life, especially as women, than at any other time in history. This makes for more thought. Our advanced technology makes for more venues for more thought. The more associated I am with unnecessary thought, the less control I have in staying awake. Engulfed in the unawareness of thought, I react out of repetitive behavior, and am susceptible to discomfort at any turn. When I am fully engaged with unmonitored thought, my life is controlled by it.

Thought Control

Thought is not to be controlled. That's like asking a fish to stop swimming. However, the less I associate to thought, the less unnecessary mental traffic I experience. In lucidity, thought needs no control. When I am lucid thought becomes the powerful tool it was meant to be, assisting Self, rather than assisting the mind-made identity. Controlling thought is impractical, but managing thought is helpful. Meeting thought with acceptance, and choosing lucidity, is the most effective thought-management there is.

The best part is that thought-management automatically leads to successful peace-management, fear-management, anger-management, and happiness-management. If there were such a thing as control, thought-management would be it.

Cutting The Strings

The greatest control we'll ever have is in cutting the puppet strings of unconsciousness.

Living inside of heedless thought is like leaving a two-year-old alone in a room. It may be quiet for a while, but eventually the Cheerios are going to hit the fan. The greatest control we'll ever have is in cutting the puppet strings of unconsciousness.

When I realize that I have no absolute control over the flow of life, I am free to surrender to the flow of my own highest good. There is no absolute control over life because we don't need it. My mind doesn't always know what to do, which way to go, or even which shampoo to buy. My Guidance does, and I'm free to choose, in every moment, to practice letting Self lead the way.

Thought can no longer control you when you know it as something separate from Self.

When you recognize that there is a stream of thought interrupting your inner connection to Self, you are awake. Thought can no longer control you when you know it as something separate from Self. When I'm awake, I can choose *for* me.

The ultimate "control" is being awake.

When I'm not controlled by thought, I'm free to communicate what's right for me. I do it in a matter-of-fact manner that implies that my truth is perfectly okay to have, and to share. What happens after that is none of my business, because my responsibility is to recognize and honor my truth. The universe takes care of the rest. I've witnessed things effortlessly fall into place. The ultimate "control" is being awake.

EMPOWERMENT:
Being in "control" is being awake, and letting Self lead the way.

DEPRESSION

The Byproduct

Which came first, the pain or the story? The story, of course. When I immerse myself in reiterating painful stories, and I believe them, I create a bad habit. These bad habits run my life if I am not awake to them. Too much thought, without the balance of being, is an invitation for suffering.

If I'm experiencing depression,
I'm living in unexamined stories.

Whenever I fall submersed into the mind's activity, I am dominated and limited by the mind's programming. It's here where the dream can turn into a nightmare. If I'm experiencing depression, I'm living in unexamined stories.

Hell is not a place, it's a belief.

Depression can be experienced as a result of being detached from Self. In depression I unnecessarily languish in a space of torment and distress. Believing consistent negative thinking is skating along the edge of the abyss. Depression is the abyss. The deeper you go, the more it hurts. The deeper you go, the less you remember who you really are. Hell is not a place, it's a belief.

Stay Out Of Whine Country

Instead of gifting myself my own wordless attention, I'm busy mentally retelling and reliving painful scenarios. I believe unmonitored thought without questioning it. Instead of waking up, I cry in the arms of the messenger of feel-bad. This is depression. And I have the power to change it.

Suffering is the pinch under the table, the warning bell that warns of unconsciousness. How can I wake myself up if I don't know that I'm sleeping? Stay out of whine country, and FUEL Your Life.

I accept where I am in the moment. Not with lip service, but with the silent burn of the experience of acceptance. Right now, it is what it is, and I am where I am. I flow the emotions that rise, by wordlessly embracing them, and watching them vanish. By giving emotion my silent, undivided attention, I allow the body to be heard, and to breath easily again.

Practice Equals Patterns

I am much greater than any feel-bad hormones that may be traveling through my bloodstream. I suffer not because I'm not good enough, can't get it right, or lost my way. I suffer because I'm sleepwalking. I'm unconscious, retelling, reliving, rehashing unquestioned negativity, and believing it.

Practice equals patterns. The more I sing my feel-bad songs, especially if they are coupled with peak emotion, I create a painful program, or pattern. I wire suffering to play in a loop, continually. It's time to wake up to the bigger picture. Often times just becoming aware and noticing this unconscious behavior, is enough to turn the ship around.

The Bigger Picture

Everything serves, if you allow it.

If I'm convinced that a situation is miserable and bleak, there's one thing I can be sure of. I'm not seeing the whole situation. Every painful situation has the seed of Conscious expansion. Because I don't see it, does not mean that it does not exist. It's there, patiently waiting for me to awaken to it. Everything serves, if you allow it.

Waking up into self-kindness is the
light that leads me out of depression.

I am greater than my unconsidered thought. I am greater than any story that my mind may tell. I am greater than my history. My well-being is my responsibility. Waking up into self-kindness is the light that leads me out of depression. It's time to practice something new, and to wire new patterns of empowerment.

I'm willing to step up for myself. I'm willing to witness painful thought, flipping it like a coin to expose all the good that I've been missing. I'm willing to let painful emotion flow and go, instead of sustaining it. I will trade negative thought for positive thought, until I can step into the peace of lucidity. These are the practices that create the most powerful patterns. They are the practices that awaken me to the bigger picture of my highest good. An authentic life of peace and joy.

EMPOWERMENT:
As the lucid eyewitness, I flow unconditionally. I awaken to the bigger picture and turn my ship around.

DESIRE

My Head Or My Heart?

Is your core desire your head's desire, or is it your heart's desire? Do you want to be a doctor because your head desires prestige, or because your heart loves to help heal people? Are you an acrobat because courageousness is the desired characteristic that your mind wants to add to its self-made identity? Or, are you an acrobat because your soul sings when you experience the joy of soaring through the air?

Innie Or Outie

*An outer desire
represents the inner desire.*

Let's slice desire into two parts. We have inner desires and outer desires. Inner desires are things like feeling loved, important, successful, or appreciated. They stand quietly in the shadow of outer desires, sometimes completely hidden. Outer desires are things like a new car, a promotion, or a new relationship. An outer desire represents the inner desire.

Honesty opens the door to clarity.

Instead of getting hung up on chasing the objects of outer desires, I prefer to cut to the chase. Do I want the promotion because I love the work, and feel a happy resonance when the idea of it pops into my head? Do I feel happy, driven, or inspired, outside of a story? Or, do I want the promotion because it would make me feel successful and important? Is my desire in support of the higher Self, or in support of the self-made identity? Honesty opens the door to clarity.

Logical Sense Or Nonsensical Joy?

The distinction between logical sense and nonsensical joy, feels like the distinction between surviving and thriving.

How can you tell if your desires are coming from your head, or from your heart? Question them. What do you desire? Why do you desire that? How does it make you feel? If your answers make more logical sense than they do nonsensical joy, then maybe your desire belongs to your head and not to your heart. The distinction between logical sense and nonsensical joy, feels like the distinction between surviving and thriving. Accept, stay lucid, and follow the scent of your own feel-good.

Surrendering

Following what feels good, or what interests you, can be a lesson in surrender. Surrendering to what you enjoy, without reason, can be a hard thing to do. We believe that we just don't have the time to partake in anything that the mind deems unproductive or illogical. The truth is, the mind just doesn't know.

I read a true story once about a guy who suddenly became inexplicably interested in photography. He surrendered to this strong interest, and indulged himself. One day he came across a flyer advertising a free local photography meeting, and decided to attend. When he got there, he found a group of mostly seniors, sharing stories about their photographs.

He decided to duck out early. As he walked down the stairs at the front of the building, he heard the door open behind him. A young woman, who was in the same meeting, decided to leave early as well. He stopped to talk to her. Turns out, they hit it off and began dating. They ended up falling in love and getting married.

Finding the right woman and marrying was something this man had deeply desired. The interesting thing is, right after he met this woman, his ardent desire to learn about photography had disappeared. Had he not allowed himself to follow his new interest, his life may have gone very differently. He let himself enjoy his newfound, inexplicable, nonsensical interest in photography, and in addition, it led him to something even greater.

Learning how to gift ourselves with the things that make us happy in the moment, is extremely advantageous. If you feel drawn to something, let yourself get a closer look. Try it. It's about how much you're enjoying it, not how well you do at it. There's always time to be happy.

Your heart's desires, outside of reason, are the crumbs that lead to the life of your dreams.

Don't worry if the mind can't figure out what you will do with your newfound ability to build bird houses out of old chop sticks. Figuring things out is not required. The only thing that is required is allowing yourself to partake in the enjoyment. Your heart's desires, outside of reason, are the crumbs that lead to the life of your dreams.

EMPOWERMENT:
I serve my soul, by questioning my desires.

DISCONNECT

Once Removed

To feel disconnected is to feel separated, or disengaged. Disconnect feels like coming close to the mark, but not quite hitting it. I feel like I'm on the outside of life, looking, but not really touching or taking it in. While loneliness is associated to being detached from other people, disconnect is a more encompassing experience. I could feel disconnected from others, as well as from my work, or even from life itself.

When I feel disconnected, I am
unplugged from Self, and lucidity.

Understanding the concept of love, and wordlessly experiencing it are two very different things. Similarly, when the sleeping mind lives in perpetual, unmonitored mental activity, the result is being once removed from life, and everything in it. You understand life, but you don't really experience it. When I feel disconnected, I am unplugged from Self, and lucidity. We are all disconnected when we are not lucid.

Reconnect

*Reconnect to Self, or life will
find a way to get your attention.*

We practice living externally, instead of internally. Is most of your attention on what's going on outside of you, instead of what's going on inside? If my focus is outside of myself, judging and correcting reality, I have deserted myself, and ultimately my own happiness. I can't find me out there, until I find me in here. Life is always pointing us back to Self. Reconnect to Self, or life will find a way to get your attention.

Do I notice my thoughts? Do I check in with my gut? What makes my insides smile? Am I reacting or responding to these questions? Reacting to life comes from the assimilated, repeated behavior of the thinking mind. The mind's reactions are based on guesswork and analysis. They produce similar or the same results, and are laced with feel-bad emotion.

*When I experience life authentically,
there is no such thing as disconnect.*

Contrary to reacting, responding to life comes from Self, the real me. The response is genuine. It is devoid of fear, reasoning, or enhancing the identity. It emerges as naturally as breathing, in pristine truth. It feels sure, right, and satisfying. It is authentic. When I experience life authentically, there is no such thing as disconnect.

My full attention is the most precious thing I have to give.

In lucidity, I am plugged in, directly connected to Self, and the Universe. I am in the field of unbound possibility. Here, I'm free to give wholly of myself, without the filter of unnecessary mental noise. I'm free to experience my life instead of narrating it from a distance. My full attention is the most precious thing that I have to give. Offering it, connects me with the people, places and things in my life. My lucid attention connects me to life itself.

EMPOWERMENT:
I reconnect to Self and life, by giving my mentally silent, undivided attention. Let the magic begin.

FEAR

Let me not forget, I am dreaming.

The Mother Of Feel-Bad

However illusionary, fear is the mother of all bad feelings. Fear, and the endless forms it takes, can rob us of wonderful life experiences. If you peel back the onion of your bad feelings, you will ultimately find fear.

Fear is an asset to survival when it is in response to the dangerous threat of becoming someone's lunch. Nowadays, we have evolved to where someone could experience a panic attack by thinking unpleasant thoughts. Psychological fear is not an asset to survival.

Limited Visibility

One day while cleaning out the cat's litter box, a sudden swoosh of knowing rose up internally. I unexpectedly recognized the many ways that fear had pervasively inhibited my life experiences. Over the years, there has been the fear of not doing well, the fear of losing something, the fear of not knowing, not being good enough, and not being able to get it right. I understood how fear had been the multi-masked culprit, that whispered lies to lure me off the road of my best life.

This realization came as one hunk of knowledge. Lucidity, or a moment of mental silence, opens the door for such realizations, even and especially when you least expect it. This realization had a profound affect on how I viewed fear and my life thereafter.

When I see life through fear-colored glasses, my life experiences are tinged with fear. My decisions become influenced by avoidance, instead of authenticity. I inadvertently bypass opportunities for growth. Life becomes about surviving.

Fear Lies

What I push aside, I drag behind.

Fear tells me that it's too painful to process my emotions. That's why when I look at something that feels painful, my reaction is to push it away, or repress it. In the name of protection or survival, the mind deems certain things dangerous, even if they are not. What I push aside, I drag behind.

Luckily, I had it up to my sixth chakra with fear's scare tactics. I took a chance. Turns out, looking directly in the eye of what I fear does not destroy me after all. It sets me free. Each time I look in fear's direction, inching up on it, I am weakening the old, fruitless programming, and teaching my brain new, empowering behavior.

Facing Fear

Your truth is the thing that you want to discover or face. And yes, sometimes the truth hurts or scares the hell out of us. Finding it and looking at it is the exit door to suffering. Sometimes the mind hides our truths and we don't easily see them. Other times, we know the truth, but we won't look.

For instance, my truth, in this moment, is that I'm petrified of being anesthetized. Having had a bad experience in the past, I know that I am afraid that I won't easily be able to come out of sedation. I notice that my body quickly reacts negatively to any thoughts about having to be knocked out, or sedated in any way. I am so afraid of being anesthetized, that some years ago I had a lumpectomy with local anesthesia, because I would not let them knock me out.

How can I drop this fear? I allow the mind to put a finer point on the fear, without falling unconscious into it. I fear that I will lapse into an anxious panic, while trying to wake up. This is the thing I will look directly at, even though I strongly feel the resistance of both mind and body. I witness the thought, and state it. *I am afraid that I will have the same experience as before, internally flailing in panic, not being able to wake up.* I then sit in complete mental silence.

Witnessing thought, is similar to being at the movie theater and making a comment about what's happening in the film. Falling unconscious into thought is the same as connecting to and believing the film so much so, that I start freaking out right there in my seat. In awareness I recognize that I am not in the movie, I am watching it.

Looking directly at my fear, I notice emotions begin to rise. I feel the fear, like subtle bursts of panic, begin to spark from the inside. I watch it with my silent attention. I notice that it quickly rides up the center of my chest, into my throat. My throat begins to tighten, and my eyes tingle as tears begin to form. The mind says, "I am afraid."

I allow the emotion to run its course. After about thirty seconds, it begins to dissipate. I just flowed the emotion of fear, as the eyewitness. I watched the experience at the same time that I was having it. I did not fall unconscious into it. I fall unconscious when the mind forgets that it is watching, and falls asleep into believing and having the experience.

Flowing this emotion, desensitizes it and enables me to look even closer. I allow the fear to thoroughly speak, feel, flow and go. I want to embrace the fear until the mind no longer sees any truth in it. Beyond the mind's beliefs, is the freedom of reality. I sit quietly. In wordlessness, realization occurs.

I suddenly recognize that I am not what's happening to me. I am That which witnesses it. The real me is outside of thought. I realize that I am okay. In the moment that I experience this realization, my fear begins to fall away. I can feel it dissipating. This is happening because the mind is not *saying* it is okay, it is *seeing* that it is okay. I'm seeing beyond the mind's belief.

***In lucidity I see reality, and in
reality everything is always okay.***

Even in the midst of a panicked mind, I am still okay. I am not the thought that's panicking, I am the one who notices it. I make the effort to lovingly embrace the mind as if it were a small, scared child, and bring it back to Self. In recognizing Self, I come back to reality. In reality, pain and suffering does not exist. I will be with me. When I am with mySelf I am outside of the stream of thought. In lucidity I see reality, and in reality everything is always okay.

Update

I am very happy to share this update with you. After over twenty years, I did the thing that I could not do. I got knocked out. Granted, it wasn't the heavyweight stuff that they use for major surgery. It was procedural sedation, also called Twilight Sleep. Still, the fear felt very real.

I FUELed myself for about a week before the procedure. I was good until a moment before the anesthesiologist plugged the sedative into the intravenous tubing. I started to feel the fear and reminded myself that outside of thought, I am always okay. I held onto being the eyewitness as my mind anticipated the feeling of the sedative kicking in. This was a possible freak-out point, but I remained outside of thought. To my surprise, I witnessed a warm, comforting feeling rising up in my body. It was not at all what the mind anticipated. It felt soothing, like a warm blanket. The pleasant surprise may have been brief, but it was clear.

I then remember hearing my name being called. I noticed feeling like I was being woken up from a restful sleep. The mind quickly remembered that this was the second half of the race. If I don't readily wake up, or if I feel too drugged, fear may swoop in and the mind may have its way with me. Groggy as I was, I held onto my lucidity. My mind stood guard and kept it's eye on the fact that, outside of thought, I am perfectly fine. And I was, perfectly fine.

Finding Your Wings

Fear is our Kryptonite. Believing fear weakens the connection to our power. Fear drains us of the joyful life experiences we came here for. Questioning thoughts and stories, and flowing the ensuing emotions, enables me to discover the fears that are holding me hostage in my own life.

Recognizing fear for what it is, may be all it takes to get your wings back.

I witness the unfounded conclusions that the mind jumps to. Even in tiny, unrecognized fears, such as the fear of coming off as curt or unkind, if I were to be honest with myself and the world. Recognizing fear for what it is, may be all it takes to get your wings back. Or, you may find the wings you never knew you had.

EMPOWERMENT:
No matter what fearful movie is showing on the mind's big screen, I am the one in reality, outside of the movie, witnessing it. In reality, I am always okay.

FOOD

Food As An Indicator

Technically food is not a life experience, but I know a few people who may dispute that. I'm one of them. Apart from its nutritional benefit, food is used for a multitude of purposes. Food has been used in art, science, healing, for comfort and of course in gestures of love.

Our present global circumstance includes multitudes of people who do not have sufficient or nutritious food to eat, despite the abundance of the planet. In this case, food or lack thereof, is an indication that it is indeed time to awaken. It is time to evolve out of the fear-based paradigm that allows us to disregard the greater good, in favor of profit and power. It's time for the evolution of our own Consciousness to catch up with the evolution of technology.

Survive Or Eliminate

Let's say that I have a manicured backyard. To keep it that way, I have two choices. One approach is to consistently make the effort to cut back the weeds, to maintain the lovely landscape. The other approach would be to remove the weed completely, root and all. This way, I would not be consistently working to maintain the landscape. I would be able to live freely and still enjoy a manicured backyard.

This metaphor represents my relationship with food. Continually cutting back the weeds, represents living my life while trying to survive an unhealthy relationship with food. Removing the weeds from the roots, represents eliminating the unhealthy relationship with food.

Starving, Binging, And Big Hats

Whether you're starving yourself, binging, or wearing big hats made out of fresh produce, food is never the culprit. My food related dysfunction is a symptom, not a cause. I eat too little food because I'm having a misunderstanding. I eat too much, for the same reason. I believe flawed thoughts, that produce feel-bad feelings. I believe that if my body were different, I, and my whole life, would be different too.

Comfort food is false freedom.

When my thinking mind and its programming changes, my relationship with food and my body will change. When I tweak the inner controls, change happens *for* me, much more than it does *by* me. Authentic change does not come with self-deprivation or self-sabotage. Self-punishment is a painful misconception. Comfort food is false freedom.

You could still lose weight, or eat healthier with the use of discipline or sheer willpower. The successes that I have had using discipline and willpower have lasted as long as the discipline and willpower, or until I resumed living in my old programming.

Cover My Bases

Bad programming that stimulates overeating is preceded by a thought and emotion, that my mind deems too uncomfortable to experience in the moment. The mind looks to its arsenal of deterrents, and launches the binging behavior in an attempt at keeping away what feels uncomfortable or painful. A temporary fix, that in the long run makes things worse.

I approach my unhealthy association to food from all three places, mind, body and spirit.

I have the power to refocus my efforts. I can take the same amount of effort that I waste being in resistance to food issues, and more effectively use it to eliminate the root cause. I work at counteracting the ill affects of my mechanical behaviors with healthy food and exercise. I also go within, using the four practices of FUEL Your Life. I approach my association to food from all three places, mind, body and spirit.

Using My Tools

When the urge to eat in excess arises, I recognize a pattern, a faulty program, a bad habit. In a moment where I seem powerless to my inner prompting, I stop, and get lucid. I come into the present moment and recognize the isness of the situation, before I unconsciously jump into obeying it. Here I am, and there is a pattern firing in my head, instructing me to comfort myself with food.

It's never personal, it's the programming.

As I wrote about earlier in "Addiction," I have witnessed my mouth begin to salivate in response to a pattern firing in the brain, prompting me to eat when I feel overwhelmed. The mind is truly a fascinating tool. It's never personal, it's the programming.

It is within that very moment, when my synapses are firing like a bad lightening storm, that I can work my most powerful skill. The skill that allows our operating system to update itself, or my ability to look at and change my own programming.

Before immediately obeying the mental prompting to eat when I'm not really hungry, I simply take a moment to do something else. Anything else will do. I could sing my favorite song, dance a little dance, or silently try to name the seven dwarfs. Every second that I take not giving in, every moment that I do something different before I indulge, the pattern skips a beat, takes a dent, weakens.

Before beginning to eat, I take a breath and get lucid. As the eyewitness to thought and emotion, I now have a guard at the gate. This keeps me from falling unconscious. I am now awake, appreciating the food, and able to slow down and savor every bite. This allows me to become satiated instead of having my eyes roll back as I unconsciously go in for the kill, only to emerge stuffed and disappointed with myself. I do not have to be a servant to bad programming, that holds me enslaved and suffering.

There's another little trick that I find helpful. Make a loose fist. This is the approximate size of your physical stomach. Before eating, I make a loose fist, turning it around to get a good look at the actual size. Sometimes I even hold it up to my abdomen, so that the mind can begin to understand what the approximate size of the stomach looks like.

These may be quick, subtle, seemingly ineffective efforts, but over time they pack a powerful punch. I have nothing to lose by doing it, except some bad, painful programming. I'd be lying if I said I couldn't do these things, even once a day. I'm lying to myself if I say that I can't practice noticing thought and emotion, so that I may recognize when a pattern ignites. I'm lying to myself if I say that I can't take a few seconds to put a small dent into the programming, before giving in to it. Every effort counts. Every effort adds up.

I can FUEL my life almost anywhere, anytime, even standing in front of an open refrigerator door, salivating. I can do some form of exercise, even if I march in place, or lift my arms up and down from a seated position. Every one of these small doable efforts are updating the programming and moving me closer to freedom. You can do it too. The question is, will you?

This is not about keeping score, it's about keeping on. I keep at these practices as often as I can. I make an effort to show up for myself everyday. If I fall down, I don't beat myself up. I just get up. It is in my best interest to keep singing that song of self-worth. These efforts are acts in self-kindness, and have produced successful results. I've learned that stepping up for myself, even in the smallest of ways, tastes better than anything.

Freedom Is Inevitable

If I am not awake to recognize bad programming, I become a servant to it.

Eventually, I see change happen. I witness myself pushing the plate away when my stomach says that it is full. I am prompted less and less to overeat, or to comfort myself with food. If I am not awake to recognize bad programming, I become a servant to it. When I notice the strong urge to partake in less than self-kind behavior, I have the chance to free myself. This is the recipe for authentic, lasting change.

The Core Desire Buffet

Before you start your day, take a moment to step up to The Core Desire Buffet. Imagine a buffet of the most wonderful life experiences. Choose a powerful item or two, and intend to experience the manifestation of these desires throughout your day.

How you come to feel confident, grateful, secure, loved, heard, happy or excited is not your concern. The experience will present itself to you in whatever way it does. Your only job is to recognize it, and savor it. These are the things that fill us up in ways that no food ever could.

EMPOWERMENT:
I am greater than my programming. Before every meal and snack, I become the lucid eyewitness.

FORGIVENESS

A Clean Slate

What does it mean to forgive? By definition, forgiveness means to drop my feel-bad feelings. It is to stop feeling wronged, angry, or sad about a person or situation. How do I do that? Do I try to see that relinquishing my bad feelings is in my highest good, and just stop having them?

It seems that forgiveness is a decision to stop telling my hurtful story. I could wipe the slate clean by deciding to forget about the incident. If I dropped the story, I wouldn't experience the bad feelings produced by it. After all, if the incident has already happened, and I still feel-bad about it today, I feel bad because of my story, not the incident. The incident is not happening now.

I could forgive by deciding to let the past be the past. But what if I still feel angry underneath? What if I still feel wronged, or hurt? What if I don't like or trust you anymore? Seems like this version of forgiveness depends on how well I could stick to my decision to outwardly keep the peace, force a smile, and greet you cordially. This is difficult for me. I suck at hypocrisy.

A Better Way

In unraveling the mystery of forgiveness, I realized that I needed to find a way to authentically drop my pain. To do that,

I would have to change my mind about the situation, not create a new story. I would have to discover a new perspective.

I took a chance at working with my reasoning, in lieu of seeing things differently. Actually, I had decent results. This reasoning tactic worked better on the smaller issues. The larger, more painful issues looked at reasoning, and smacked it in the mouth. At best, reasoning temporarily reduced the heat, but did not alleviate the more hurtful situations.

> *To find my truth and set myself free, I must be willing to do the thing I couldn't do.*

I tried putting myself in the other person's shoes, and hoped that empathy would carry me the rest of the way. That doesn't cut it if I'm angry about the incident. If I have anger, I know hurt is hiding behind its skirt. It's hard to empathize with someone who my thinking mind feels has wronged me in some way. I have learned that my peace, freedom and growth are on the opposite side of the door that I refuse to enter. To find my truth and set myself free, I must be willing to do the thing I couldn't do. My thinking mind hates that.

I view the situation as the objective eyewitness. I'm willing to see the isness of the situation, outside of my mind's version of it. I accept unconditionally. This does not mean that I like or agree with it, it just means that I acknowledge and accept what is. I allow myself to feel whatever emotions arise, until they melt away, unimpeded by the thinking mind. Finally, for my own well-being, and in some cases the well-being of others, I exercise lucidity.

Truth And Freedom

When Jesus said, "Father, forgive them, for they know not what they do," he was talking about unconsciousness.

If someone is acting out of fear, or their own pain, they are unconscious. They are sleepwalking with limited perception and recognition. They are trapped in their own painful stories, even if their actions seem intentional, or born out of jealousy, hurt or anger. They are separated from God, from Self, from reality. This is unconscious behavior. When Jesus said, "Father, forgive them, for they know not what they do," he was talking about unconsciousness.

Unexamined thinking becomes the filter that obscures truth.

Someone who is submersed in and believing a fear-drenched, angry or painful story, is temporarily incapable of seeing the actual isness of the situation. Unexamined thinking becomes the filter that obscures truth.

The clarity of a situation, outside of the mind's interpretation of it, sets me free. This, of course, includes my part in the situation. I must be willing to be honest with myself. I must be willing to see what else is also true about the situation, in exchange for my own growth and freedom.

> *There is only the misunderstanding*
> *of truth, and the freedom of clarity.*

Once I recognized unconsciousness as a state in which one does not see things as they really are, I realized that there really isn't anything to forgive. There is only the misunderstanding of truth, and the freedom of clarity.

I Choose Love

Sometimes the clarity of truth reveals more than blameless misunderstandings. I may realize that your fear-based, unconscious thought was the devil that made you do it. But, you did do it. So along with knowing that you're unconscious, I know that this is what you do. Now the ball is in my court.

If this negative behavior was a one-shot deal, finding clarity often strengthens a relationship. However, if intentional negativity is a person's repeated behavior, continuing the relationship becomes a matter of self-worth. The next time you do it to me, it's my fault. You and reality are kind enough to tell me what you do. I'm either awake to it, or not. I may love you, but I love me too. I can love you without letting you stab me in the back, repeatedly. Self-kindness is my responsibility. Self-kindness is my priority. I move myself to a safe place from which I can love you, without being interrupted by your unconscious, negative behavior.

No one can hurt me unless I allow it. For me to allow it, I must join them in their unconsciousness.

Falling submersed into unmonitored thought, is to disregard what I am. It is to disregard that I am in a benevolent construct. No one can hurt me unless I allow it. For me to allow it, I must join them in their unconsciousness. I choose to do my best to stay awake. I choose to recognize that we are each a piece of Divinity, sometimes sleepwalking in fear. I choose to realize that unconsciousness knows not what it does. I choose to love you, and myself.

EMPOWERMENT:
They know not what they do. They are unconscious.

FREEDOM

Around We Go

Life wants out of the box.

Life wants out of the box. Living in the box called thought, with its programmed actions, biography, and beliefs, make for a cramped existence. Meanwhile our true Selves wait patiently to be noticed. Our true Selves send messages as dreams and ardent desires. The thinking mind reasons them away.

Discomfort comes to alert us to our unexamined reasoning, and to guide us back to our longings. The mind mistakes the discomfort as something to avoid and complain about. Around we go. We don't stop until we wake up.

Freedom Is Clarity

You can choose your soul's freedom,
over enhancing your mind's identity.

Here in this place we call life, freedom is clarity. Getting clear may require stepping outside of your comfort zone, to recognize your truth. You have the power to choose to be forthright with yourself. You can choose your soul's freedom, over enhancing your mind's identity.

> *Witnessing thought, flowing emotion,*
> *exercising lucidity, and unconditional*
> *acceptance, are the practices that lead to clarity.*

This human experience is not about becoming someone or something. It's about unbecoming, so that we may discover our true Selves, and experience the joy of authenticity. Witnessing thought, flowing emotion, exercising lucidity, and unconditional acceptance, are the practices that lead to clarity. In clarity, what is not necessary falls away.

How much clarity are you experiencing? Do you resist your emotions? Do you beat yourself up? Do you focus on the negative, lay blame, or lie to yourself? Are you walking around in the employ of a mind-made facade? All of these activities are done within the confines of unconsciousness. They obscure the clarity of the truth, and it is our truth that sets us free. You can choose authentic freedom.

Authentic Freedom

As the eyewitness to my own thinking, I recognized things about myself that made the thinking mind cringe. I recognized where I was neglecting myself, lying to myself and beating myself up. I noticed worry, blame, and serving the mind-made identity over my higher Self.

The occasional sting of clarity is a small price to pay, to experience the kind of authentic freedom it yields. Noticing the mind run its programs and tell its stories, allowed me to examine thought and flow connected emotion. This allowed me to drop the pattern of overlooking my opportunities and hanging on to painful emotions. That's a freedom that cannot be bought, but it can be found.

In authentic freedom, I do not have to say yes to you, if it's at the expense of saying no to myself. I'm free from the unnecessary burden of pleasing and appeasing. I'm free from self-sacrifice, and the fear of disappointing others. Authentic freedom is being kind to myself. Being kind to me, is being kind to all.

*In pursuit of freedom, the
body can be used as guidance.*

I use the body like a compass. The thinking mind may lie, or fall asleep into its own thinking, but the body is always truthful. If I'm not sure if I'm lying to myself, or making the right decisions, I place my silent attention on the body. When I am looking in the direction of clarity and fortuity, the body confirms this by spontaneously loosening up. Muscles I didn't even realize were contracted, release and soften into a comfortable, reassuring position. In pursuit of freedom, the body can be used as guidance.

The Key In Your Pocket

Freedom from the misunderstanding that I'm not good enough, releases me from the anguish of trying to disprove it.

Freedom from the misunderstanding that I'm not good enough, releases me from the anguish of trying to disprove it. Clarity tells me it was never even true to begin with. Life feels easy and enjoyable without learned prejudgement. Freedom is allowing our true Selves to spontaneously respond to this life experience, instead of being the mouthpiece of memorized behavior. Genuine freedom is to have this human adventure without carrying the burden of shame, guilt, sadness or fear. How wonderful to authentically meet the people, places and things in my life with open arms, a silent mind, and a direct connection. We hold the key to our own freedom.

EMPOWERMENT:
Awakening is the ultimate freedom.

FUTURE

The Illusion

Just as tomorrow isn't real until it is today, I am living life on the outskirts of reality, until I am lucid.

Living for tomorrow isn't one of my best ideas, because tomorrow never comes. It's always today. Today used to be tomorrow, when it was an illusion. It is the present moment that brings the illusion into reality. Just as tomorrow isn't real until it is today, I am living life on the outskirts of reality, until I am lucid.

Checking Out

Tomorrow is nothing but a thought.

Whether we call it wondering, wishing, or worrying, we are checking out, into an illusion called the future. Tomorrow is nothing but a thought. I'm not saying that a happy fantasy, or planning for the future is a bad thing. I'm saying that some thoughts regarding the future aren't in our best interest. How can I tell the difference? As the eyewitness, I spot an unnecessary contemplation of the future, when it results in a bad feeling.

*If I want to effect my future, I
work on my rote behavior today.*

Happy daydreaming is all good until the dream turns bad. If I find myself living in or for the future, I'm abandoning myself. I soon begin feeling disengaged and detached. If I want to effect my future, I work on my rote behavior today.

*I may only have now, but how I'm
having now is what creates my future.*

What is more important than when or where I am, is how I am. I flow emotion, to avoid the ball and chain of dragging it around with me. I practice unconditional acceptance, so that I don't stall out in opposition to what is. I become the lucid eyewitness, making myself available for guidance and opportunity. I may only have now, but how I'm having now is what creates my future.

What-Ifs

Occasionally I find my thinking mind wandering around in the future, licking its lips at the buffet of what-ifs. We sometimes live in fear of what hasn't yet happened. We unwittingly trade the joys, sign posts and peace of the present moment for the fear of the unknown future. When looking at this practice in awareness, it seems crazy. In unconsciousness, I venture into the future where I forego happy for sad, peace for chaos, feel-good for feel-bad.

> *When we make friends with the*
> *uncertainty of the future, our real power*
> *starts to create our highest good, right now.*

The mind reasons that it contemplates a future in an attempt to prevent what it does not want to happen. Despite that, we attract what we focus on. We end up living in avoidance of something that we have no concrete way of knowing will even happen. We live in a field of endless possibility. What sense does it make to live in fear of a few possible outcomes, when there are an infinity of possible outcomes? When we make friends with the uncertainty of the future, our real power starts to create our highest good, right now.

EMPOWERMENT:
There's no more powerful way to effect my future, than FUELing my life today.

GRATITUDE

The Power Of Gratitude

Find your gratitude,
find your power.

In the midst of what seemed like chaos, I struggled, but managed to find a small piece of gratitude. I held it tightly in my hand. I focused on that tiny piece, and before long found another. Focusing on those pieces of gratitude, I found even more to be grateful for. The magical cohesion of these small pieces kept me afloat. Before I knew it, I had the power to find happiness in the midst of chaos. Find your gratitude, find your power.

There It Was

In the "Life Purpose" chapter of this book, I share an experience that I had at a weekend workshop. I wrote, "Elation was filling me up and spilling over." The morning after I returned home from this workshop, I sat alone at the dining room table. Everything looked the same as it did before the weekend, but it felt inexplicably different. The mental silence felt so good, that all I wanted to do was just be. I sat there, in wordlessness. I felt full, fulfilled, satiated, on a deep level. I was suspended in the most pleasurable state of profound peace, awe and great joy.

When my thinking mind put its attention on these feelings, I could feel them expand and well up inside of me. My body suddenly felt like a fragile container, that I knew could never house the full vastness of this experience. Instead of bursting, I cried. "Elation was filling me up and spilling over."

I remember wondering if I had lost my mind, sitting there in mental silence, crying tears of joy for seemingly no good reason. There was no story, so there seemed to be no reason to feel that much joy, and yet, there it was.

A Real Thanksgiving

I felt joy, profound peace, aliveness, and excitement. It seemed as if every good feeling was swirling around inside of me, all at the same time. Oddly enough, if I were to give this cornucopia of emotion only one name, I would have to call it *gratitude*.

My mind didn't know what to make of that. All those intoxicating, wonderful feelings, when melded together felt like the deepest gratitude I had ever experienced. Although surprised, I wasn't going to question the gift horse. I sat in bliss.

Any one of us can move closer to this wonderful experience simply by choosing to focus on what we have to be grateful for. Not lip service, but really feeling it. Not just occasionally, but enough to create a powerful new habit.

Focus Equals Destination

*Go beyond the concept of
gratitude, into the experience of it.*

Think of some wonderful thing that you are grateful for, and in mental silence, feel it thoroughly. Feel it down to your core. Go beyond the concept of gratitude, into the experience of it. Without the mental description, notice and feel.

Our minds are running all day. We either notice what we're thinking, or we sleepwalk through it. It takes the same amount of energy to pay attention to the things that make me feel good inside, as it does to pay attention to the negative things. Where are you habitually putting the spotlight of your focus?

Power Brush

In the morning, while brushing your teeth, notice three things in your life that you are grateful for. Whether it's gratitude for your loved ones, or for your new toothbrush, it doesn't matter, as long as you're honest and sincere about it.

*Putting my focus on a thought, especially
when coupled with peak emotion, is what
ignites it with the potential for manifestation.*

Quieting the mind, and viscerally enjoying the feeling of gratitude, tells the Universe that I want more of this experience. What I focus on, expands. Putting my focus on a thought, especially when coupled with peak emotion, is what ignites it with the potential for manifestation. When I feel grateful, the Universe reflects back to me more things and experiences that I can be grateful for. The key is to be open to whichever way it manifests into your life. Get out of your own way. Look for what makes you feel grateful, like there's a reward for it. Oh boy, is there.

EMPOWERMENT:
I venture beyond the concept of gratitude, into the magical experience of it.

GRIEF

The Transparency Of Grief

Grief is a draining experience. We know it as anguish, heartache and mourning. Whether we grieve a person, pet, career, or even a long-lost waistline, grief is a painful story. What if my story was incomplete, or a misconception?

To alleviate grief, I don't have to eliminate beliefs, or talk myself into believing something different. It's about seeing that my belief is not absolute, and recognizing it in a new way. It's about widening my view to take into account what I'm not noticing or what I'm forgetting. When I'm able to see what I'm overlooking, grief becomes transparent and I see it as an unnecessary illusion.

The Mercy Of Clarity

When I awaken from pain into unconditional acceptance, I open the door to the mercy of clarity.

When I'm grieving, I am having nonessential thought. This is thought that is not necessary for me, my health, or my survival. I'm having a nightmare. When I awaken from pain into unconditional acceptance, I open the door to the mercy of clarity. As stated earlier in Part Two, unconditional acceptance does not mean that I have to like something, agree with it, or want it. It simply indicates that I acknowledge what already is.

> *When we forget or don't notice*
> *what else is also true, we suffer.*

Going beyond the concept, into the experience of unconditional acceptance, opens the door for peace, healing, and understanding to rise up from within. The truth is always there. When we forget or don't notice what else is also true, we suffer. Relinquishing resistance frees up energy that I could be using to heal in acceptance.

I Can't Lose What I Am

Only in a confused, unconscious mind can loving someone or something equate to suffering. The mind sees death or change as personal loss. This belief hurts, to alert me to its untruth. My grief isn't really about a person or thing. It is about me, and the belief that I am now missing part of myself, part of my identity or my joy. How could this be true if I'm still able to experience the same love and happiness now, that I experienced when this person were here in the room with me?

> *I suffer for no other reason*
> *than my own awakening.*

We resist the belief that our lives may be different after a loved one passes. While it may be true that life is different in some ways, it is not true that I'm losing something that will mar or permanently disable me. Although grieving may certainly feel like it, the incident of my grief will not prevent me from ever being happy, whole, productive or purposeful. Only unconscious, fear-based thought can do that. I suffer for no other reason than my own awakening. There is no truth in suffering in the name of authentic love.

To experience grief, I must momentarily trade gratitude and love for untruths and resistance.

Recognizing the mind's untrue beliefs may not totally exempt me from the experience of grief. It means that I have a better chance at witnessing it, and processing the experience in a healthy way. We are all able to do this. To experience grief, I must momentarily trade gratitude and love for untruths and resistance. In lucidity and acceptance, it is possible to meet the changes of life without losing mySelf. I choose to celebrate the joy of our everlasting connections.

Unbreakable

When I feel able, I make the effort to refocus. I look for what the pain has obscured. I see that life is change, a continual flow of energy. We are meant to move with it. In order for me to grieve, I must stand still and step out of the flow of life. In awareness, I slow down for the mind and body to catch up with the eternal flow of life. I allow the body to say its piece by wordlessly flowing emotion. I hold this healing space in lucidity.

The body is the vessel, and the mind is the operating system. I am the life energy that animates them. I am eternal. I am energy, changing form and never dying. In grieving a loved one who has passed, I recognize that they are not their body. We inhabit the body to have this life experience. We then flow on. We never end.

We go home, vacating this temporary body. We are energy. Energy does not need a vessel to exist. Nor do we need a vessel to connect. In that, we never lose each other, or the joy we feel from our eternal connection. The love and joy that I have for my loved one when they are seated across from me, is the same love and joy that I have when they are in a different room. I still possess the same love and joy when they have vacated the building, as when they have vacated the body. There is no loss. Loss is a painful misunderstanding.

My loved ones will always be with me, whenever I place the focus of my attention on them. I am not my body, or my thinking mind. I am That which is. Our connection is unbreakable.

EMPOWERMENT:
Grief is the messenger sent to remind me to awaken to the connection of eternal love, once again.

GUILT

Either End

Guilt is a versatile little piece of unconsciousness. It can be experienced in many ways. Guilt can be a weapon, a deterrent, a means of manipulation, an excuse, or an obstacle. I've even read guilt referred to as both healthy and unhealthy, in terms of remorse versus retribution.

When we believe we did something that we should not have done, we call ourselves guilty. When we believe we did not do something that we should have done, we call ourselves guilty. Believing the story that puts me on either end of guilt, puts me at a disadvantage.

The Source

The mind formulates the story of guilt by believing that someone or something is responsible, in a particular way, for my pain. The mind looks outside of itself for reparation or for ways to alleviate the pain. Meanwhile the source of the pain is the story, not the external circumstances.

When I get caught up in believing the mind's details about why life did not go the way that it should have, I miss the bigger picture. I miss the mind in action, assigning the story of guilt. It is when I awaken to witnessing the mind's actions, that I recognize how the mind uses guilt to charge others, or a circumstance, with the power to hurt me, or to control me and my feelings.

While it may be true that so-and-so really did such-and-such, it is not true that anything external controls my life experience. Only my mind's focus, thoughts and beliefs can do that. So I suffer at the unwitnessed, unnecessary and unquestioned activity of the thinking mind. The unnoticed mind will continue to do what it does, reassigning guilt to what it disagrees with.

What You Don't Know Will Hurt You

When I believe that someone or something is guilty of a horrible offense against me, it stuffs me further down into unconsciousness. The deeper I go, the more painful it gets. What irks my thinking mind even more, is believing that someone got away with what they've done. That's a story line that morphs the hurt into full-blown anger. It took some elbow grease and repeated attempts, before I was able to see through the belief, that someone had gotten away with something. Ultimately, there is no such thing as getting away with anything.

Even if a person shows no remorse, they are still the person that is unconscious to the degree that they would act so unkindly to self and others. The Universe will continue to mirror back their beliefs and actions, often as difficult or painful life experiences. We cannot hurt another without hurting ourself.

> *Unconscious thought hurts self*
> *as unwittingly as it hurts others.*

When we are unaware, or unconscious, nothing is personal because we are sleepwalking inside of fear-based thought. Suffering is an equal opportunity experience. Unconscious thought hurts self as unwittingly as it hurts others. We can evolve out of our own suffering, or from causing suffering to another. To do that we must be willing to pass through the burning truth of our own unconscious thought and actions.

What You Do Know Will Free You

> *We cannot access That which is*
> *greater than the thinking mind, if we do*
> *not venture outside of the thinking mind.*

When we are awake, we do not have the need or desire to come from unkindness. Reality tells me that if someone does something hurtful to me, knowingly and purposefully, they still do not have the power to hurt me. That can only come from me. They either awaken false beliefs and resistance that I already have, or they don't. If they do, they allow me to rid myself of the pieces of my own unconsciousness. It is my opportunity to awaken, and move into my own empowerment and evolution. We cannot access That which is greater than the thinking mind, if we do not venture outside of the thinking mind.

One more note on the importance of what you do know. You know that we only hurt ourselves, or each other, in unconscious thought. Forgiving, or recognizing that clarity does not require forgiveness, does not mean that I will put myself in harm's way. I can forgive, or gain clarity about a murderer, but that does not mean that I will sleep in their cell.

Finding Home

It hurts when the mind disagrees with truth, and how things happen or not. It hurts me to think less of myself or to wish harm to another. I don't have to like the reality of the situation, to ask myself what else about it is true. I'm free to rest in faith that life unfolds in its own way, in its own time, and that it is in the highest good of all, even if my mind can't see it.

As this benevolent construct
hosts chaos, it hosts my awakening.

I am free to accept the isness of the moment, flow my emotions, and to reconnect with Self in lucidity. With self-love as leverage, it's easier to walk in the right direction. We are all doing the best we're able, where we are, and with what we have in the moment. As this benevolent construct hosts chaos, it hosts my awakening. FUELing myself, being willing to be mistaken, and being honest with myself, are the powerful tools that elevate me.

EMPOWERMENT:
The story of guilt alerts me to unconsciousness, and the opportunity to facilitate my own evolution.

HAPPINESS

Where Is It?

The other day I opened the refrigerator door and searched like crazy for the tofu in the green container. When the mind predetermines what something looks like, it looks for that image, and overlooks what is right in front of its eyes. I missed the tofu right there in front of my face, because it was in a *blue* container.

Well, hold on to your Tupperware, because here comes an ah-ha moment. The thinking mind does this with almost everything. We're sleepwalking, dictating to the Universe what everything is supposed to look like, and how it's supposed to show up in our lives.

We're so preoccupied with what's going on in our heads that we miss many opportunities. Happinesses are right under our noses. The mind overlooks what it says it desires, because what it desires shows up in a different package than expected. It's funny when you stop and really look at what the mind does. Not ha-ha funny, because at the end of each day, we keep coming up short. When I'm lucid, I'm on the other side of the fence of that ceaseless mental dictating. I'm open and available to recognize all the delicious things staring me right in the face.

Mind Over What Matters

*When we settle, the mind chooses something
other than what the soul is longing for.*

Noticing that you're unhappy is a sign post pointing at being trapped in unexamined thought, or resistance. Are you settling for the stinking leftovers when you really want something new, hot and different? When we settle, the mind chooses something other than what the soul is longing for.

Our insides say one thing, and the mind says something else. The thinking mind swoops in with fear-based reasoning that says some is better than none, or something familiar is better than the unknown. The mind simply has no way of being absolutely sure that what it is saying is true, or will be true. So fearful thought decides for us, and we end up blaming someone or something outside of ourselves for the unhappy outcome.

The Default State

*Happiness is our default state
when we honor our truths.*

So I settle. I settle for little things, and I've settled for some big things. The thinking mind does this because it's trying to protect me in some way. It means well. I appreciate that. Unfortunately, when we act out of fear, even just tiny fears, we are not honoring our truths. That's what this is all about. Happiness is our default state when we honor our truths.

> *If the decision feels good,*
> *it's a go. If it feels bad, it's a no.*

Short of throwing out the new shoes, junking the car, or burning the couch you settled for, how do you begin to honor your truths? As the eyewitness, I notice the mind in action. I catch the mind when it makes a decision, and I can weigh that decision against my gut. If the decision feels good, it's a go. If it feels bad, it's a no.

The New Way

You can start with the small things. Notice what you really like or prefer, without exception or reason, and share those truths in a pleasant way, even if it is just with yourself. *I don't feel like eating that, but I'd love some of this…. That sounds good, and I'd prefer to go here instead…. I like dance music, maybe we could compromise…. Thank you for inviting me, no, I won't be attending.*

It's never about what you eat, where you go, or the music you listen to. It's about recognizing what your insides long for, as opposed to what the mind settles for or desires. When we get good at honoring what makes our guts smile, we will witness life catering to us. Practicing lucidity helps to keep me out of the old programs of fear, forfeit and sacrifice, so that I may install the new and empowering habit of living my truths.

***It's not about getting your way,
it's about finding your way.***

Realizing and honoring what makes your gut smile may feel difficult or awkward at first. Once you experience how fabulous it is to glide through life on your truths, you'll be welcoming the chance. Seeing the difference between what makes my insides happy, and what the mind was going to settle for, changed everything. It's not about getting your way, it's about finding your way.

Don't ask your mind, ask your soul.

What if I'm not sure what makes me happy? Don't ask your mind, ask your soul. Make yourself available to answers that manifest in lucidity, not supposition that comes out of reasoning. With practice you will be able to tell the difference between the mind's fear-based guessing, and the truth that your soul whispers. You'll know the whispers of your soul by how they make your innards quiver with happiness.

> *Put your silent focus on your insides and*
> *teach the mind what being happy feels like.*

Follow what feels good, right, joyful or exciting. Follow that in blind faith. Let go into it, without the restrictive naysaying of the thinking mind. Experiment. Get out there and see for yourself. Follow what feels good to your soul, and pay attention to what that feels like emotionally and physically. Put your silent focus on your insides and teach the mind what being happy feels like.

The Happiness Quotient

Self-worth is a determining factor in the happiness quotient. In the name of moving forward, let's realize that we not only deserve to be happy, no matter what, but it is our responsibility. If I'm not happy, I'm sucking the oxygen out of the room for everyone else. The people and things in my life can't help but mirror my unhappiness back to me. It's not them, it's me. Instead of just letting the thinking mind make fear-based decisions, create a new habit of noticing what makes you happy, and then do the best you can to honor that.

The Gift That Keeps On Giving

Like I always say, realization is a gift that keeps on giving. I bet you think that recognizing yourself unconsciously denying your truths, and forfeiting authentic happiness, is groundbreaking enough. It gets even better. The extra added bonus is that every time we honor our truths, even in just silently acknowledging them, life feels juicier and sweeter. These are the acts that wake us up to self-love.

Honoring our truths is not just about getting happy. It's about getting closer to Self, until we are living in the bliss of authenticity. The higher Self always knows the way. That's why when we honor our truth, everything else ends up working out for the best. Happiness points the way.

EMPOWERMENT: The way to real happiness is in waking up to, and honoring our truths.

HEARTBREAK

Clearing The Smoke

We get caught up in the smoke, instead of trying to put out the fire. The fire is the story that creates the experience. The story of heartbreak is extinguishable. I am not suggesting that the betrayal did not happen, or that the physical death did not take place. I am not attempting to diminish the severity of, or argue the existence of one's pain. In awareness, we can find our way out of pain, and grow in pleasure.

> *Heartbreak is not a measuring*
> *stick as to how much I love.*

There's pain in the misunderstanding that something has changed and lessened me in some way. Things may be a bit different, and change is the constant of life. It is the natural, flowing way of it. Waking up out of heartbreak is self-kind. Heartbreak is not a measuring stick as to how much I love.

> *I am the only captain of my ship. I'm*
> *either at the helm, or have abandoned it,*
> *and am being tossed around in rough seas.*

If I believe that someone or something is responsible for making me happy, or taking away my pain, I'm setting myself up for an inevitable letdown. That would imply that someone or something outside of myself controls me and my experiences. This is not true. I am the only captain of my ship. I'm either at the helm, or have abandoned it, and am being tossed around in rough seas.

It's natural to feel compassion, to miss someone, or to feel the pangs of rejection. The pain is amplified by the fear that I will no longer be okay, or that I will be without something that I need. If I don't have it, I don't need it. Escorting the thinking mind into lucidity clears the smoke, and allows for the healthy processing and healing of what breaks our hearts.

On The Mend

I will meet the experience of heartbreak with loving kindness. I will embrace the pain in an attempt at seeing through fear and resistance. Instead of waiting around for time to heal my wounds, I choose something better. I choose what's self-kind. I choose to use my tools.

Coming into the silence of the present moment offers tranquility, in contrast to the infliction of pain-producing thought. In lucidity we approach unconditional acceptance. It is what it is in the moment. There is no additional dialog required of me to accept the isness of the moment.

Flowing the emotions of heartbreak, in mental wordlessness, is the equivalent of Self wrapping its healing arms around me. As long as I stay out of a story, I am lightening my emotional load. When I fall into the painful story, more negative energy and painful emotion is created, adding to the load and reinforcing my anguish.

I sit in the silence and allow emotion to emerge. I allow any tears to flow, fists to clench, or my gut to wrench. I honor the feelings that arise by watching them without evaluating, judging or attaching to thought. The emotion will crescendo, and melt away. When it does, there's no denying it. It often feels like someone lifted a cement block off of my chest, and it is usually accompanied by a spontaneous, deep, purifying breath.

I can choose to place my focus on the love that I have, instead of the fallacy of loss. I can focus on the appreciation of having had something or someone that I enjoyed. I can appreciate the discovery of what is not right for me. This makes me available for something much better. Gratitude is a cure-all that offers immediate solace. None of these feel-good choices require anyone or anything outside of my lucid focus. I am awake and aware. I am on the mend.

EMPOWERMENT:
I choose to use my tools to awaken from heartbreak and come back to Self. This too shall pass, and I know the way.

HURT

Time To Awaken

Hurt notifies me of my own unconsciousness.

If there's one thing I can be sure of, it's that the Universe has my back. The emotion of hurt is a merciful messenger. It squeezes me so that I may awaken to find and remove the splinter of my misunderstanding. Hurt notifies me of my own unconsciousness. Feeling hurt tells me that I oppose something, or that I have inadvertently overlooked truth. It's to let me know that there is an opportunity to be had. The mind has taken the isness of a situation and made it personal. Hurt says, *Sweetheart, it's time to awaken*.

Hurt is the disapproval of reality.

We want to change what hurts. The thinking mind thinks that it, and the thing that hurts, are two separate things. What hurts me in this moment, is the desire to change something. Hurt is the disapproval of reality.

We believe something must change to be happy again. I may not enjoy what happens, but I will find a way to accept that it is, in this moment. Beyond the theoretical understanding of unconditional acceptance, awaits the burn of freedom.

Freedom from hurt does not mean that I don't care, that I have forgotten, or that I don't love. It is to remember that God or the Universe, does not require the help of the thinking mind, to unfold in the highest good of all. My mind's unwillingness to see beyond my story, is the resistance that holds me captive. When I hurt, I flail against the ceaseless flow of change that is this human experience. I'm bearing the crushing white waters, by holding on to the branch of resistance, anger or fear. In acceptance I go with the flow. I heal, grow, find gratitude and reap its bounties.

A Better Way

> *In wordlessness, I witness*
> *what the body wants to say.*

The anguish of hurt, makes flowing emotion my first stop on the wake-up trail. While letting emotion make it's way to the surface, my only job is to make sure that the flow is unimpeded by thought. I may witness my teeth grind, as anger erupts like an inner volcano. I may grieve, mourn or sob. I witness it all rise and fall. This is the silent flow of emotion. It is not a retelling of a story. In wordlessness, I witness what the body wants to say.

Once I let the body "speak" by letting emotion flow, those energies become transformative. The positive possibilities are endless. I have experienced peace, appreciation, and freedom. I have met with fortuitous blessings, and have seen situations change right before my eyes.

The Mirror Of Opportunity

> *Hurt says that I am not
> seeing the whole picture.*

I remember once offering a bit of encouragement to a friend. She rejected it by telling me that she didn't ask me for it. She didn't ask me for my opinion, or for what I may think would be helpful. She told me that sometimes all people want to do is to tell their story, and that compassion is all that should be offered. I immediately took it personally. I apologized, but felt angry and hurt. Hurt says that I am not seeing the whole picture.

This experience pointed at reflexive behavior that doesn't always serve me or others. Once I was no longer in the throes of hurt and its big brother, anger, I was able to see that I did offer unsolicited encouragement. She was right about that.

I believed the thought that as a friend, relative, mother, or even just a sentient creature, I should always try to offer help. I now see that only in lucidity, from the prompting of my higher Self, can authentic help be offered when it is authentically needed. Turns out, this was a very freeing realization for me, but only when I was willing to look past the hurt, and see myself through it.

*Life is a mirror. It allows Self to speak
to me through everyone and everything.*

This was an opportunity for my programming to take a look at itself. When I realized that, I realized that the incident wasn't personal after all, even though at the time it sure felt like it was. It's never personal. Life is a mirror. It allows Self to speak to me through everyone and everything. Only I can know what the message is, by turning down thought and listening for truth. Truth resonates in an undeniable way. Rest assured, somewhere in what hurts, lies the opportunity for empowerment.

Rise

*A hurtful situation is a
realization that hasn't happened yet.*

If I don't learn from my suffering, I will repeat it. If I reach inside of hurt and learn from it, I will emerge free and empowered, much like a phoenix rising from ashes. A hurtful situation is a realization that hasn't happened yet.

EMPOWERMENT:
Reach inside of hurt and learn from it, emerging free and empowered, much like a phoenix rising from ashes.

ILLNESS

Double Trouble

I now recognize the extremely painful experience of a double kidney infection, as a series of wake-up calls that went unanswered. It started as a tap on the shoulder. I ignored it. I didn't see it at the time, but I had been pushing an enjoyable, but very heavy schedule. While venturing out into blissful territory, I built a momentum that I did not want to interrupt.

About two weeks later I ended up with a hospital stay, of which I cannot remember the first three days. On the fourth day I opened my eyes, both figuratively and literally. The doctor told me that if I would have waited four more hours before going to the hospital, I would have never made it to the hospital. Point taken. I knew that all of this could have been avoided, and what's worse is that I was the one who failed to avoid it.

I wanted nothing more than to get back to my regular daily life. I was humbled, and used the lesson to take a closer look at myself. Even too much of a good thing, is not a good thing. It's not a good thing when doing is not balanced with resting and being. This painful experience helped to get me back on track. Even within an enjoyable time of your life, the thinking mind is capable of whipping up a big dose of double trouble. If I'm not visiting lucidity enough to spot it, unmonitored thought can put me out.

The Antidote of Consciousness

When I live in untrue beliefs and resistance, I live in discomfort. If I continue to ignore the discomfort of unconsciousness, the Universe will eventually flag me down with something that I can no longer ignore. I was amazed to learn how quickly I could poison myself with a cocktail of resistance and false beliefs.

Witnessing thought, and the subsequent negative feelings, prompts me to stop and examine that thought. If I'm willing to be honest with myself, I'm able to see through negative thinking. I can spot my own unconsciousness and in so doing, I awaken. When I'm not willing to reevaluate my own beliefs, or to allow emotion to flow, I'm destined to live within the confines of its negativity. The negativity continues to become more painful, sometimes manifesting as illness.

Feeling bad is the heads-up that I'm veering off the path of my highest, healthy good. Being the eyewitness allows me to recognize when I'm tired, so that I can choose rest over the unkind thoughts that push me farther than I should go. I recognize which thoughts and emotions are unkind to self.

I notice feeling rushed, so that I may slow down. I perceive saying yes, when I really want to say no. I notice being judgmental, upset, sad, angry, or overwhelmed, and realize that I have fallen asleep in thought. Thought that is unnecessary to my well-being.

> *When you honor the truths that*
> *your soul tells, it is supported*
> *by the power of the Universe.*

I've learned that no matter how scary honoring my honest truth is, it is the very thing that has offered me freedom from mental, emotional and even physical pain. It is that important. When you honor the truths that your soul tells, it is supported by the power of the Universe. There's no obligation to publicize your truths, unless you are authentically moved to do so.

The purpose that illness serves is subjective. It may be a sign post, or an escort into realization. Illness may be an invitation to practice unconditional acceptance, to be the eyewitness to thought, or to flow emotion. These practices reconnect us with the power of Self. To a thinking mind, they can be called both an antidote, and a preventive measure. Joy, healing, peace and freedom can be found on the journey inward.

EMPOWERMENT:
Illness is a prompting to check my connection to Self. Accept and reconnect.

INSPIRATION

A Mission Without A Story

Inspiration is the magic that kisses you on the cheek, and opens the gate to the flow of effortless creativity.

Inspiration, divine or otherwise, is sublime. The energy of inspiration is often invigorating and exciting, even if it may not look like that on the outside. As an artist, I have spent time in the silent space of inspiration, and know it to be wonderful. Inspiration is the magic that kisses you on the cheek, and opens the gate to the flow of effortless creation.

Inspiration, a mission without a story.

When I do something from authentic inspiration, it feels like a sudden and compelling flash of motivation. I feel it driving me from the inside. There's no mental reasoning or discussion. There's no doubt. Whether inspiration comes to clean out the junk drawer, or to change the world, I accept gratefully. I move forward with focus and passion. Inspiration, a mission without a story.

*Authentic inspiration feels as
wordless and natural as the pull
between a magnet and metal.*

Your mission, should you accept it, is from your higher Self. Simply quieting the mind and living from the inside out, makes you available for inspiration. Authentic inspiration feels as wordless and natural as the pull between a magnet and metal.

Let Loose

Unmonitored thought is the fork in the road. This is where I can get sidetracked by the fears, and second-guessing of the thinking mind. I must witness, but not attach to the mind's contemplations. With each passing thought, I give myself the benefit of coming back to lucidity, so that I may feel my way through. If I don't do these things, I run a high change of falling asleep on inspiration.

*Let your heart sing like no one's listening,
and your soul will dance like no one's watching.*

Inspiration silently rises like a sweet fragrance. It can lend itself to any endeavor. It has nothing to do with discipline or willpower. When inspiration sweeps you up, allow yourself the reckless abandon to thoroughly enjoy it. Allow yourself to surrender to it. Stay out of the mind's negative discussions. Let your heart sing like no one's listening, and your soul will dance like no one's watching.

EMPOWERMENT:
Letting your gut lead the way, in acceptance and lucidity, opens the door to inspiration.

JOY

The Hankering

The human experience is the cat that chases the string called joy. We are fascinated by this feel-great experience, as we dream about it, long for it, and work our way toward it. Sometimes we grab at joy in desperation, and occasionally we lose all site of it. No matter what our many endeavors look like on the outside, somewhere in their core lies the hankering for joy.

> *I had been in pursuit of joy*
> *on the outside of myself, while*
> *it snuck up on me from the inside.*

It wasn't until I experienced sudden moments of satori or kenshō, which loosely translate to brief moments of insight or enlightenment, that I understood the dissimilarity between mind-made joy and authentic joy. These moments of joyful bliss, made clear the place from which real joy arises. I had been in pursuit of joy on the outside of myself, while it snuck up on me from the inside.

The Distinction

Authentic Joy lives outside of reason.

Most often, happiness comes with a story, or for a reason. Authentic Joy lives outside of reason. Experiences such as happiness, enjoyment, pleasure, delight or satisfaction, can be derived from outside of myself, while authentic joy emerges from within.

*The ability to connect
to Self, is self-evolution.*

I don't make this distinction to say that happiness is lesser than, or not good enough. I site the distinction between happiness and joy, to point to our innate ability to experience joy independently of external circumstances. That we do not regularly experience independent joy, indicates that we have an ability that we do not use, a skill we have not yet developed. The ability to connect to Self, is self-evolution.

My Well

Authentic joy is the wordless essence of what we are.

Rarely is the thinking mind quiet long enough to experience the welling up of joy. Ongoing mental speculation acts like clouds blocking out the sun. The sun, like joy, is always there, just temporarily obscured. In lucidity and acceptance, joy is experienced in the journey. When we find joy in the journey, we find the creative flow, inspiration, and our highest good. Authentic joy is the wordless essence of what we are. The quieter the mind, the better connection I have to the still, quiet Joy that I am. In connecting with it, I stream and radiate joy into this life experience.

Self is my never-ending well of source. It is a well that only I can find, and only I can drink from. When I'm able to maintain that connection, I experience something that goes beyond the meaning of the word *joy* as my mind knows it. Authentic joy awaits.

EMPOWERMENT:
In connecting to Self, I connect to, and open the flow of authentic joy.

LIFE PURPOSE

I Want That

One day, as a kid, I was poking through stuff in the attic. Buried under a pile of old newspapers and magazines, I discovered a hand rendered sketch that immediately captured my attention. Someone had drawn a woman, wearing what looked like a wedding gown. I kneeled down for a better look. I admired how the pencil markings were meticulously applied in all the right places. I appreciated the details that spoke of an ornate and beautiful fabric.

It was a lovely sketch. For some reason, to me, it was much more. It was fascinating. I wasn't wishing that I looked as pretty as the girl in the sketch, or about getting married one day. In that moment, more than anything, I wanted to be able to draw like that. Not only to draw like that, but to draw that, people in clothing, odd as it seemed. Eventually, that's exactly what I ended up doing. I would later call apparel design my life purpose, simply because I loved it so much.

Denial, Resistance And Discomfort

After college, I warmed up to designing for retail. I couldn't wait to get up in the morning to start my day. Despite the hectic, deadline-driven environment of the apparel industry, I savored it. I felt certain, purposeful, and effective.

After years of loving design, it was as if the Universe reached in, snatched my favorite drawing pencil right out of my hand and said, "You won't be needing this anymore." Things slowly started to change. While the enjoyment of my work started to inexplicably fade on the inside, the fashion industry started to fade on the outside. Garment manufacturers, textile mills, screen printers, and trim vendors, started going out of business. Things got weird. Then, things got tough.

Without a full-time designing position, I spent the next few years freelancing. I was in denial, resistance, and discomfort. Why would this happen? What did I do? What didn't I do? I couldn't figure out why I couldn't get back to that luscious space that I had once been working in.

The Impetus Of Truth

Denial is an ingredient for stagnation.

Eventually, I started noticing how bad I was feeling every time I went on an apparel design interview, or got a new freelance client. I was prolonging my discomfort by making excuses why I was feeling bad, instead of recognizing the feel-bad as an actual sign post. Denial is an ingredient for stagnation.

It was a long time coming before my mind finally took its hands down from over its eyes. I finally recognized, and admitted to myself, that deep down inside, my truth was that I really didn't want to design apparel anymore. The thinking mind didn't know what to do with that, as being the designer was a huge part of its identity. I could not deny that I felt completed, totally satiated with designing apparel, and my insides were pulling me in a different direction. The problem was that I didn't know in which direction that was. Denying all of this was the source of my discomfort.

After realizing my truth, the mourning period was temporarily alleviated by my new adventures in graphic design. I then began the search for my next life purpose. The time was laced with sadness, hope, and an underlying current of fear.

I spent more time on spiritual growth. At one point, I attended a weekend workshop where I had an experience that I later wrote about in an article titled, *A Funny Thing Happened On My Way To A Life Purpose.* The collective experience was one of Conscious expansion and clarity. This changed everything. I share it with you here:

A Funny Thing Happened On My Way To A Life Purpose

For the past several years I had been hot on the lookout for my elusive life purpose. I had already spent many years of my life doing what I believed I was meant to do, until it was time for me to move on from that, to something new. I never anticipated doing anything new. I didn't know how to do that.

In an attempt to find the spot I am meant to stand in, I read books, meditated, filled notebooks with written exercises, tried new things and even went back to school. Every time I thought I was getting close to identifying what my new life purpose could be, my new endeavor would turn a bit sour and the trail would run cold. I felt like I was running in place.

I worked on listening for and deciphering the steps my Guidance was urging me to take. It took some time to get my thinking mind to stop trying to identify each step I took, and in haste, label it as some kind of new career, or life purpose. I worked on letting go, and going with the flow, even if I had no idea where it would lead.

I decided to "surrender" to the Universe and to my Higher Self. I didn't want my thinking mind to decide what my life purpose should be by conjuring one up with nothing more than its logical deduction. After all, a thinking mind never knows for sure. I believed that no matter what my purpose is, once I find it, I will know it by the vast joy I feel, no matter what it turns out to be. My Higher Self is the one that holds the GPS to my best life. It's holding the compass to what makes my heart sing. And what makes my heart sing are the sign posts that lead to the life of my dreams. I wanted one of those.

I attended a weekend workshop with the intent of eliminating the obstacles, if any, that would account for my seeming stagnation and lack of direction. I wanted to clear my own runway for takeoff. In retrospect, I can see how my experiences during this workshop weekend were all crumbs that led my way home.

A funny thing happened to me on my way to a new life purpose. During one of the workshop exercises we were all lying on the floor on our backs, chanting to music. I had never chanted before, and just went along for the ride, stepping outside of my comfort zone as another means of growth. I could feel the vibration of sound in my chest. I could feel that vibration being blended by means of the blending of our many voices. It was at this moment I experienced something very profound.

Despite having been fervently searching for my life purpose, in this moment I had never before felt more like I was exactly where I was supposed to be. The experience went beyond the words I use to describe the knowing that I was doing exactly what I was meant to do, in this moment, lying in a circle on the floor. For it was in that space that I lost myself and experienced being an anonymous part of the whole. This was it, this was home. Being an anonymous part of the whole was the most natural feeling space I had ever been in. I had clicked into place. It was wonderful. No, it was much bigger than wonderful. I felt like a fountain that was overflowing in the most beautiful way. As I experienced what felt like water overflowing, or something pouring out of me, it produced the feeling of elation. Elation was filling me up and spilling over. How could I ever want to be anywhere else?

Happily, the afterglow of this experience stayed with me for a full week. I still had no idea where I was supposed to be, or what I was supposed to be doing. Only this time, it didn't matter. I was too preoccupied with basking in the lingering elation I had been so vehemently chasing, the elation I believed could only be found in a life purpose. The fear of not finding what I was ultimately looking for was gone. I had been wearing the ruby slippers all along.

I had been going about things backwards. It's never about the "what." It's always about the "how." No matter what I do in this life, as long as I'm taping into my Source, I will flow the happiness that I am made of into that endeavor.

Imagine that. We spend our lives wondering how we could "achieve" our happiest life, our little "heaven on earth." Most every one of us, having been pointed in that direction, search outward. My experience told me I had been looking in the wrong places. There is no happiness outside of me.

The degree to which I experience happiness is the degree to which I have touched the happiness that I am. The happiness I experience in this place I call life, is flowed from within, outward. If I am cut off from that place, or can only access a small portion of it, that is the extent to which the happiness will be reflected and experienced in my life. The journey only looks like it's on the outside of me. The journey is within. This is my life purpose. You'll now find me traveling an enjoyable ride, where ever it leads, mapped out by my inner GPS, my Guidance. I will be the one wearing the ruby slippers.

EMPOWERMENT:
Our collective life purpose is to awaken into the bliss of an authentic human adventure.

LONELINESS

The Recipe

Think about a time when you were discovering a new relationship. Do you remember getting to know this person? Did you notice the nuances of their expressions, observe their emotions, appreciate stories of their successes? We develop meaningful relationships by connecting, by giving our undivided attention, observing, noticing, and sharing.

The less undivided attention, caring and sharing that I give to myself, the more I create the recipe for loneliness.

The more I fail to notice myself, my thoughts, emotions, desires and joys, the farther I grow apart from Self. The less undivided attention, caring and sharing that I give to myself, the more I create the recipe for loneliness. If I feel lonely, it is because I am not connecting with Self. The real me, outside of the identity.

Mirror Mirror

> *I cannot expect others to give me*
> *something that I'm not willing to give myself.*

Life mirrors my disconnect. Not connecting with Self in a loving way, is what is reflected back to me in my life experience. I cannot expect others to give me something that I'm not willing to give myself. I am worth giving myself all of me, my loving, compassionate, undivided attention. The relationship I cultivate with Self, is the relationship I cultivate with others.

Plug In

Unconditional acceptance empowers me. I may not like loneliness, but accepting the isness of feeling that way, empowers me to do something about it. Accepting, allows me to move into change. What am I resisting? False beliefs and denied emotion, that eventually become the obstacle that I cannot get past.

Witnessing thought, acceptance, and the wordless flow of emotion, does the trick. Taking one tiny step at a time gets you closer and closer to freedom. You don't have to fling yourself outside of your comfort zone. You could stick one leg out at a time, until you warm up to it.

Practicing lucidity offers me a chance for an authentic and unfiltered experience with the people and situations that I encounter. It plugs me in. If I want an authentic relationship with someone, I plug in and cultivate an authentic relationship with Self.

My Own Best Friend

Some people need to be told, some people need to see, and others need to feel someone else's affection toward them. Have you noticed which you prefer? Knowing this can help you get good at being good to yourself.

Whichever works best for you, kind self-talk, a present, or a soft blanket and permission to take a nap, do what makes you feel good, happy, and comfortable. Become grateful that you are such a good friend to yourself. You will begin to notice moments of self-appreciation that feel so good that you'll savor spending time with yourself.

EMPOWERMENT:
In self-kindness, and the joys of self-love, there is no such thing as loneliness.

LOVE

Toot Toot

Love must be one of the most overused words in any language. It's wielded around, and applied to as many people and things in our lives as possible, regardless of its diluted significance. Nevertheless, we regard love as so important, that it makes the world go 'round.

To some, love may mean to obey, excuse, or enable. To others, love means as many things as they could get out of their stretched imaginations. If we collected all the wedding vows ever exchanged, we'd have the start of a long list of definitions and descriptions for love.

I hate to keep tooting the same horn, but this is a place of duality, which means that love is a two-sided coin. There's unconscious love, and there's the real thing. Love can be experienced in two different ways.

The higher Self is unconditional love.

Love is not something the higher Self needs or wants. The higher Self, or That which I am, *is* love. Self is not just any kind of love, it is the one true love. The higher Self is unconditional love.

When I experience love that comes with a story, even if the story tells of boundaries or expectations, that is love that is asleep in the dream. It has conditions that say I will love you as long as you comply. When I love with no story or conditions, that is love that is awake in the dream. Awakened love is unconditional love.

Me Too

That's not to say that you must put up with anyone's shenanigans, not even your own. You don't have to be a doormat, or stay in any relationship that your guts, not your head, are telling you to move on from. If I feel fine when I think of you, but my wordless gut says that I need to go, then I know that going is my truth. If I feel anger, or hurt when I think of you, then I know it's me, and I look to self for misunderstanding and opposition.

The degree to which I am unconscious, is the degree to which I am separated from love.

Practicing lucidity opens the space for the love that we are made of, to flow freely into this life experience. The less mental gridlock, the less of a filter between myself and love. The degree to which I am unconscious, is the degree to which I am separated from love. In awareness, I can love you, and love me too, unconditionally.

Falling In Love With Who?

Falling in love can be the most wonderful feeling in the world. Why is it that the feeling of love seems to fade or disappear? When I fall in love unconsciously, I am falling in love with who I think someone is, not necessarily who they really are. Who is he, really, outside of his self-made identity?

I meet who his mind thinks he is, and he meets who my mind thinks I am. We're both unaware that our authentic Selves live just outside of the self-made identity. When I'm unconscious, I see his self-made identity through my history, learned behaviors, filters, stories and beliefs. Two unaware people meeting, is like being at an amnesiacs-only costume party.

Who am I without my labels, expectations, boundaries, and descriptions? That is the Me from which I love unconditionally.

Who am I, really? Who am I outside of my mind-made identity? Who am I without the fear? Who am I without my labels, expectations, boundaries, and descriptions? That is the Me from which I love unconditionally.

The Greatest Love Of All

*The spiritual journey begins to blossom
into a blissful love affair with Self.*

The spiritual journey begins to blossom into a blissful love affair with Self. So what does Self got, that self hasn't got? It's what it doesn't have that makes all the difference. The higher Self has no conditions because it recognizes the illusion. It recognizes the innocence of unawareness. It recognizes that unconsciousness knows not what it does. It loves, no matter what.

*Self-love is the pinnacle of the human
adventure. The greatest love of all.*

Self-love is the mother of all love. I must love myself from the inside out. The love that I share with others are bonus gifts. The amount of self-love that I have, is the amount of love that I'm able to give to others. The greater my self-love, the more love is reflected back to me in my life experiences. Loving others, teaches me how to love myself. Self-love is the pinnacle of the human adventure. The greatest love of all.

EMPOWERMENT:
Awakened love is unconditional. I practice unconditional love, for self and others.

MEDITATION

Check-Out Check-In

Being lucid, even sporadically, is a meditation. Doing anything you love, in mental silence, is a meditation. Being in the creative flow, is a meditation. There is also the more traditional meditation, that requires the task of spending time in nothingness, or sitting in awareness. Meditation is the experience of being awake and aware.

Meditating, in any manner, opens us to the stream of Consciousness. It allows us to step out of the commotion of mental busyness, and frees us to acknowledge our gut, our guidance. Meditating, even for a brief moment, is like plugging in for a powerful recharge. Life flows more easily and effortlessly when I balance doing with being/meditating.

We are capable of checking-out of thought, and checking-in to a cerebrally quiet space at any time. Granted, some thought-filled moments are more difficult to step out of than others. Although it can be covered up by mental noise, nothing can affect this quiet, inner space. It's always accessible, and always there, inviting thought to notice.

Fuel Your Meditation

When I first began the more traditional meditation, where I sat still and silenced the mind, I could only sustain it for a few moments at a time. Still, I tried. I worked on it a little everyday. Once I got the hang of it, I began to experience how good meditation really feels.

Thought is like a pebble, thrown into a perfectly still pond. Attempting to resist thought, causes it to persist, as the adage goes. So, I FUELed my meditation with the two practices of unconditional acceptance, and being the eyewitness.

> ***I am the eyewitness, peacefully watching the leaves of thought float quietly downstream.***

As I sit silently in awareness, I become the eyewitness. I notice thoughts that pop into my head, without focusing on them, attaching to them, or falling submersed into them. I "watch," as an objective eyewitness, in total acceptance of what is. The mind moves out of the way, so to speak. I notice a thought come up, and let it float by, like a benign leaf on a slow moving river. I am the eyewitness, peacefully watching the leaves of thought float quietly downstream.

When I find the mind attached to a thought, and not easily able to let it float by, I adjust the spotlight of my concentration. In other words, to get back to the space of being the objective eyewitness, I put my silent focus on my breathing, a sound, a smell, or physical sensation that is there in the present moment. I continue to return my focus to one of those things whenever a thought pops up. Even in a quiet environment, you will notice that there is still so much happening in the now, that usually goes unobserved. Now is the time to notice.

After getting comfortable with this practice, I discovered that the mind had less thought activity. I still meet thought in meditation, and most often am able to let it float by. Some days there is more thought than others, and it feels more difficult to slip into that blissful state of inner silence. I accept that, with no opinion. Meditation goes with the flow of unconditional acceptance.

EMPOWERMENT:
FUELing my life is the living meditation of authentic living. Plug in and power up.

MONEY

Out With The Old

If money is a problem, then somewhere, when addressing a monetary issue, I'm falling unconscious. When the subject of money comes up, I'm unwittingly rerunning the same old programmed beliefs that don't benefit me. Not noticing these thoughts keeps me caught in the same loop, that keeps me in the same financial situation.

I may hold hidden beliefs that say that I don't know how to handle money, or that learning more about money would be too painful. Because of this, the mind may regard big money as a burden and as something to avoid, as it buys its weekly lottery ticket. The mind's beliefs trump luck, hope, and hard work.

If I believe that there is not enough money, ultimately I will have the experience of not enough money, *no matter how much money I have.* If I view money through the filter of unworthiness, even if my lip service says differently, the filter of unworthiness will override my efforts. When I witness my thoughts and beliefs, I uncover what my mind really thinks about money.

The Root

The cause of the lack of money may look like its due to extra expenses, or losing a client or a job. Understanding that my outer life experiences mirror my inner beliefs and feelings, allows me to address the weed at the root. The root is thought.

I began noticing how many thoughts I was having, that supported the belief that I did not have enough money. Although the higher Self knows that believing is seeing, the mind believes that seeing is believing. So I didn't just talk about it. Instead, I noticed all the abundance and good fortune that was already in my life. The more the mind saw it, the more it believed it. That's the point. I wasn't trying to prove myself wrong about money. I was opening the mind to truth that was always there. Truths that I wasn't seeing. The old programming can't argue with what the mind sees.

I also recognized an inner obstacle. I had to learn to do something that was hard for me to do. I had to learn to receive. To receive with open inner arms, instead of that weird feeling that unworthiness creates when someone, or the Universe, tries to give you something.

The more I allowed myself to receive with nothing more than gratitude, the more I experienced serendipitous events. Opening myself up to receiving, became a mental and visceral practice. For me, this practice was key. I was doing the thing I couldn't do. Even as a mental dress rehearsal. This created real change.

Refocus

Focus is my magic wand.

While the mind may overlook running water, a dozen pair of shoes, or even a stuffed refrigerator, these are all valid and true examples of abundance nonetheless. The truth is that these abundances were in my life all along. I didn't notice them because the unmonitored mind was focused on what it believed it was missing. My mind was busy in unquestioned, contaminated thought about scarcity and limitation. Focus is my magic wand. What I point at, I get more of.

When the belief in my own abundance outweighs the underlying beliefs of scarcity, unworthiness, or even bad luck, I will have changed my life experience. So while I make the effort to notice and feel the many abundances in my life, I also question the thoughts and beliefs to the contrary.

As the eyewitness I notice thought that results in self-denial. I catch the falsehoods that say that I need more than a simple *thank you* to accept abundance in my life. I flow the uncomfortable emotions, from the stories of scarcity and unworthiness.

When I witness feel-bad thoughts regarding money, I make note of them. These are the beliefs and stories that are either untrue, or those that I am in resistance to. These are the beliefs to question. These are the beliefs that lack the bigger picture.

Listing The Bigger Picture

One of my beliefs was that money equals freedom. To see a bigger picture, I made a list of how many places in my life that I already had a plenitude of freedom. I examined each of my beliefs about money, listing previously overlooked options, and real life instances to the contrary.

Let's say you hold the belief that you do not know how to handle money. List all the times that you handled money very well. Every occurrence counts. In addition, list available options you have that you may have disregarded. For example, you could educate yourself on how to better handle money. You could hire an expert in the field, instead of pressuring yourself into thinking you have to be your own accountant. What are some of your beliefs about money? What else is true, and what options or ideas have been overlooked?

Outside of the confines of unmonitored thought, lies the field of infinite possibilities.

Once on paper, it's much easier to see the ridiculousness of some of these beliefs. Some false beliefs topple like a house of cards, and others need a few kicks in the knee caps to be dismantled. If no additional truths or contrary insights emerge, intend and allow for them to pop in. The more you practice lucidity, or lessening unnecessary mental noise, the easier it is to receive these spontaneous insights. Outside of the confines of unmonitored thought, lies the field of infinite possibilities.

EMPOWERMENT:
Money is a reflection of inner thought and belief, and Self is the never-ending source of abundance.

OVERWHELM

Inner Chaos

When things are mounting up outside of myself, it is because things are mounting up inside of myself. My outer life reflects the inner chaos. I experience circumstances that feed the overwhelm.

As the eyewitness, I catch the mind as it fabricates fear-based thought. The thoughts share the same theme of not being able to accomplish what my mind thinks I must. I notice thought that says, *I'll never finish in time, I could never pull this off*, and workaholism's favorite lie, *I'm going to have to work on this all night*.

It's Not My Job Man

Life does not need my mind's assessment for it to continue to flow.

The unconscious and constant act of mentally assessing everything, produces the experience of overwhelm. I don't have to mentally assess or address everything in my environment. It's not my job to do all that. Life does not need my mind's assessment for it to continue to flow. In unconditional acceptance, I'm able to let go of that exhausting habit.

I look at my plate to determine which things are really not mine to address, so that I may scrap them off. It is in my best interest, and in the best interest of others, to recognize what is not my responsibility. There is no truth to the belief that I should be able to do it all, or that a superwoman flies solo.

Overwhelm is my opportunity for change.

In lucidity, I flow with a quiet mind, as opposed to feeling the pressures of the thinking mind's negative voice-overs. As the eyewitness, I recognize unhelpful thought and disregard it. In addition, perhaps I could ask for help, delegate, or just say no. To endure overwhelm is to believe the untruths that persuade me to disregard myself. Overwhelm is not something to endure. Overwhelm is my opportunity for change.

Easy Does It

Doing one thing at a time, in a calm and focused state, is doing my best. I will not be so unkind to myself, as to believe that it should be any other way. Get lucid, prioritize, and move. I work at reprogramming myself to do one thing at a time, with all of my attention.

Slow down, I'm in a hurry.

I learned this empowering adage from my best friend's mom, "Slow down, I'm in a hurry." Rushing and scattering my attention not only causes overwhelm, but it creates a bad habit, and that rash you get when stress turns into anxiety. Easy, does it too.

The Win-Win Way

A destination is only as good as the ride I had getting there.

A destination is only as good as the ride I had getting there. If I completed something half dead, having been overwhelmed and twisted up every step of the way, how could I have enjoyed it, or delivered my best work? My best, most enjoyable work is done in that peaceful connection to Self. The more overwhelm I feel, the farther away I am from Self. The simpler and more peaceful life appears, the closer I am to Self. Unneeded mental congestion is what sets me adrift.

If you are not willing to see it another way, you won't experience it another way.

What is in my highest good, is in the highest good of all. Don't just understand it, test it. Do what's self-kind, and move forward in peace. Drop the belief that you should accomplish more than you really can, or that you must do more than one thing at a time. If you are not willing to see it another way, you won't experience it another way. We give all of ourselves, when we offer our full, peaceful attention in the moment. That's the win-win way to savor the ride.

EMPOWERMENT:
In peaceful self-kindness, I awaken, refocus, and let it be easy.

PAST

A Watering Hole

The past is an intangible record of our lives. It is the place to which we look for our memories, and contemplate our history. The past is the thinking mind's frequent watering hole. When I could use a quick pick-me-up, it is helpful to pull a few empowering memories from the past. I choose the happiest, funniest, joyful memories, in the name of high-vibes and positivity.

The most important aspect of my trip to the past is remembering to get the hec out of there, and back to the moment at hand. Reality is in the present moment. My life is happening now. Living in the past is like driving while only looking into the rear view mirror. Eventually there is going to be an unpleasant surprise.

Time Travel

Wouldn't it be helpful to be able to go back in time and collect the gifts, lessons and empowerments, of unopened realizations? Fortunately, the past's unopened realizations are not lost or forsaken. The four perspectives of FUEL Your Life, open the space and possibility to retrieve previously unrecognized realizations. It's like being able to go back in time, seeing and experiencing the same incident in a completely different way.

The most beneficial way to look to the past, is as the detached eyewitness. This is the awakened perspective, free of the mind's filters, such as anger, sorrow, or fear. To see the past as it were, I would see it devoid of the mind's conjecture, disapproval or judgement. I'd see the past in its unbiased isness, as if I were watching strangers.

> *When I look to the past from a place*
> *of lucidity, time is no longer a barrier.*

From this awakened perspective, I also recognize my own unconsciousness. If there are any residual emotions produced by my past misconceptions, I allow them to flow. I alleviate myself of the burden of carrying a load of unnecessary discomfort any farther. The past may be an illusion, but it's still ripe for the picking. When I look to the past from a place of lucidity, time is no longer a barrier.

Changing The Past

> *When clarity offers me the truth of*
> *the past, I experience healing and*
> *freedom right here in the present moment.*

The clarity of realization shows me what really happened. It illuminates what I may have failed to notice, or what I may have ignored or denied. In clarity, I see what else is also true, for me, or for the situation. With clarity, the past changes. This is especially helpful if I'm walking around today, with yesterday's pebble in my shoe. To realize the truth of the past, outside of the mind's interpretation of it, can be life-changing. When clarity offers me the truth of the past, I experience healing and freedom right here in the present moment.

EMPOWERMENT:
I am not the content of my past. I am something much greater.

PEACE

Rubber Gloves

We define peace as the absence of war, disagreements or hostility. Peace is also defined as serenity, tranquility or stillness. Even tranquility is described as being free of disturbances. The thinking mind assigns words to explain peace and believes it knows peace. The mind does the same thing with situations, people, and even love.

We experience things through the filter of analytical understanding. The mind understands words and their meanings, combines them with learned connotations and associations, and believes it really knows something. That's like experiencing velvet through rubber gloves. While that's what we're used to, and maybe even all we know, there is something much more.

The essence of peace goes far beyond our analytical understanding. No matter how quiet we are, there is no peace if inside of ourselves we are submersed in thought and resistance. Going beyond the words is to experience the peace of lucidity.

To experience authentic peace, is
to wordlessly connect to Life itself.

Stepping out of the filter of thought, to connect with the energy of Consciousness in and around us, allows us to remove the rubber gloves and to experience the true essence of peace. To experience authentic peace, is to wordlessly connect to Life itself. This is the peace that Jesus spoke of, the peace that surpasses all understanding.

Inner Peace

What if our lives weren't led by fear, sadness or pain? We'd have more time to partake in the peace that's abundantly available from within. Peace lives in the wordless silence, that's perpetually under the layer of unnecessary thought. Peace is the feel-good of silence.

In lucidity, I embody peace.

Authentic peace is part of the inexplicable. The experience is comforting and soothing. It feels expansive, open, natural and freeing. Peace feels like a total and delicious surrender into a perfectly loving presence. Living in a world with inner peace is one of the biggest changes you will ever enjoy. When I practice lucidity, I experience less of a mental barrage of thought. In lucidity, I embody peace.

Peace is also a byproduct of unconditional acceptance. Peace melts my contracted muscles, and produces a feeling of safety and security from within. It is relaxed well-being, a calm that resonates from my core. The less unneeded mental activity, the more peace I experience. Following what feels peaceful, points me to providence.

Outer Peace

*Peace comes to me,
when it comes from me.*

Peace lives inside of me. It is not dependent on anything outside of me. If the connection to Self is clear, I know peace. My life experience mirrors this back to me. Peace comes to me, when it comes from me. Peace in, peace out.

What you feel, is what you get.

When the rough seas of thought disrupt my connection to Self, my life experience reflects this unrest. Unrest comes to me when it comes from me. War in, war out. What you feel, is what you get.

Global Peace

*If we all strengthen the connection
to the peace within our own inner
climate, the world will reflect that.*

I invite you to frequent the stillness of lucidity, so that you may go beyond the words into the experience of authentic peace. It's always with you, under the mental traffic. It's waiting for you. If we all strengthen the connection to the peace in our own inner climate, the world will reflect that. The world will change before our very eyes. Indeed, it's time to awaken into authentic peace.

EMPOWERMENT:
Underneath the mental noise, unconditional peace awaits. In lucidity I connect to the peace that I am.

POWERLESS

It's Not What It Seems

The mind sees power as some sort of attribute to be added to the mind-made identity. The more power acquired, the less potential for suffering, and the more possibility for pleasure. That's the belief, but of course that's not the truth. There are people who are considered very powerful, and yet have great suffering in their lives. The unconscious and fear-based struggle for power, has been the precursor to a global history scared with anguish and disaster.

Authentic power is That which I am, Self.

Authentic power is not an attribute. Authentic power is That which I am, Self. It rises from within, and does not require a story. It is the power of peace and higher intelligence. It is the power to create positive change. This power lives outside of unawakened thought and beliefs, in perpetual abundance. We are the very thing that the mind mistakenly believes it must attain.

Unnoticed thought is the static that festers into fallacious beliefs.

Conceptually, I understand how I am never really separated from Self, or real power. What disconnects me is the stuff that gets caught up in between. Thought is the stuff that interferes with my connection to that power. Unnoticed thought is the static that festers into fallacious beliefs. These beliefs manifest as painful life experiences. When I live in the shadows of illusionary beliefs, I feel powerless.

The thinking mind asks how it can attain power, and contemplates what it wants to do with it. The real question is, *What would my authentic Power like me to do?* This is the road that leads to authentic peace and happiness. In relinquishing the belief of having to attain power, we find the Power that carries us to the life of our dreams.

Power Up

I turn down the interference of fear-based thought. I ask my heart what it's longing for, without restriction. I watch for Self to point the way toward what is favorable, by following what feels good, soothing, or healing. I weigh new ideas in my gut, instead of only reflecting on them with mental reasoning. I have continual access to these powers. They cannot be taken away. They can only be overlooked in unawareness.

Honoring my truth is the supreme self-kindness.

There is yet another power, also readily available at any given moment. The Universe happily supports this feel-good charm. The mighty power of self-kindness. Honoring my truth is the supreme self-kindness. Whenever I discover and support my truths, I am moving with the flow of my own benediction. How do I know? It feels right. It feels good. Something favorable happens. I have fun. I may even discover a life of my dreams, that I didn't see coming.

Rescued

The scrapings at the bottom of the barrel of depression, once contained the story of being powerless. Allowing unmonitored thought to stagger through depression into a story of powerlessness, is a toxic cocktail. Believing depression when it tells me that I really *don't want to* make anything better, is not as painful as believing powerlessness, when it tells me that I *cannot* do anything to make things better.

Consciousness is only a realization away.

Deep fear rises up on the heels of such an excruciating lie. Fear and pain become your champions, rushing in to reawaken you to your own invincible power. Pain gives us the opportunity to wake up from unconsciousness, and the misunderstanding of powerlessness. Pain reminds us to quiet feel-bad thought, and to step into the power of Self. Consciousness is only a realization away.

The Winning Combination

I am never powerless. In witnessing painful thoughts, I awaken, and turn down, or turn off the incessant mental rant. Focusing on any sensory stimuli in the present moment, helps to keep resistant thought at bay. Thought recedes, and the body responds with peace and calm. By maintaining awareness and a quiet mind, I connect to Self, my never-ending source of power. If action is required, I will experience inspiration emerge from within, outside of reason.

Self is the abundant, eternal source, and lucidity is the space of boundless possibility.

To frequent the space of my own power, I witness thought, flow emotion, and practice lucidity in unconditional acceptance. Self is the abundant, eternal source, and lucidity is the space of boundless possibility. I could never lose with such a winning combination.

EMPOWERMENT:
In lucidity, power is what I am.

PRESENCE

Sliding Into Home

All of a sudden, I found myself experiencing my regular life almost as if it belonged to someone else. I slid over into this space of joy. Everywhere I looked, in all the same old places, I felt gratitude, happiness, and a subtle buzz of excitement. As the song goes, it's almost like being in love.

Presence is where the fear of the unknown, is replaced with the excitement of the unknown.

I saw higher intelligence, everywhere. Everything perfectly in its place, in its perfect time. It was similar to childlike awe. The kind of awe that you give yourself to fully. Presence is where the fear of the unknown, is replaced with the excitement of the unknown.

Presence is acknowledgement without evaluation.

Presence is a state of being. It's effortless. There is minimal to no thought activity. Presence is acknowledgement without evaluation. It is noticing without opinion. Presence is shields-down, arms open, free-flowing vulnerability. It feels like flying without a net, and realizing what authentic living is really all about. Presence, even intermittently, is bliss.

Dissecting Presence

Presence is a natural flow of emotion, in unconditional acceptance, while witnessing everything in lucidity.

If I were to dissect presence, what would I find? I found four truths that occur with no effort on my part. Presence is a natural flow of emotion, in unconditional acceptance, while witnessing everything in lucidity. When all four practices of FUEL Your Life meld together, they create that shift into the effortless and delicious state of being, called Presence.

Outside of the state of Presence, I make the effort to incorporate these four practices into my daily life experience. Inside of the state of Presence, they happen automatically, naturally, effortlessly and gloriously.

Finding Home

FUEL Your Life
F - **F**low emotion
U - Accept **U**nconditionally
E - Be the **E**yewitness
L - Step into **L**ucidity

EMPOWERMENT:
Presence is the effortless flow of emotion, in unconditional acceptance, while witnessing life in lucidity. Presence is our natural state of bliss.

PROBLEMS

The Wake-Up Call

*The farther away from Self I drift,
the bigger the wake-up call.*

When we begin to swim against the current, the Universe taps us on the shoulder to wake us up. Often times we refer to the tap on the shoulder as a problem. The farther away from Self I drift, the bigger the wake-up call.

Slowing down and zooming out to witness the story of the problem, instead of flailing helplessly inside of it, allows me to keep one foot in reality and to stay awake. When I'm able to look at the problem from the outside, as if I were witnessing a stranger's situation, I unlock the door for realization to step in. I become available to higher intelligence. I don't fall asleep into taking things personally. Suddenly the problem reveals itself as a valuable lesson or opportunity.

Pinball Wizard

Problems are like the little paddles in a pin ball machine, that influence and guide the ball one way or the other. If the paddle hits the ball just right, it can propel the ball in an advantageous direction. I'm the little ball, and my problems are the paddles that guide me one way or the other.

What determines my direction is my state of being. If I am submersed in thought, I mistake the situation as threatening, or as an obstacle to moving forward. Seeing something as an unfavorable problem, instead of as a sign post or an opportunity, puts me at a disadvantage.

What If?

When I don't witness thought and emotion and just have and believe it, the mind sees problems as bad news. What if everything does happen for a reason? What if everything does serve to further, free and heal?

I know how things go when I sleepwalk through a problem. The mind stands in unawareness and bad feelings, looking outward for reasons and blame. What if I moved into my other circle, shifting into awareness? What if I allowed unscrutinized emotion to flow, and witnessed thought as if someone else had just said it? What if I accepted the isness of whatever is in the moment, and waited in lucidity for realization to lovingly greet me with open arms? What if I tried things a different way?

When Opportunity Knocks

> *Honoring my truth always propels*
> *me in the most powerful direction.*

Let's look through the eyes of opportunity. A problem may be an opportunity to take a stand, or to choose what feels right, over what is expected or easy. A problem is my opportunity to choose what is self-kind. Identifying and honoring my truth is the best place to begin. Honoring my truth always propels me in the most powerful direction.

> ***When we find our truth, we find our way.***

Truth is what rises from within. It is not formulated thought, or a story. Truth is Guidance, not reasoning. Truth is what my higher Self reveals, when it can squeeze a word in between the flow of ceaseless mental evaluation. Truth is what the body responds to in a loosening, positive, relaxing way. When opportunity knocks, let your truth answer. When we find our truth, we find our way.

Truth Versus What's True

There is also the truths of the thinking mind. This is a bit confusing because these truths are misunderstandings or unfounded beliefs. I call them truths, but they are merely what the mind believes is true for me in the moment. Fear tells me to look away from some truths. The mind judges, and pushes away momentary truths that it deems ugly, or diminishing to the identity. If in this moment I feel a tremendous distaste for someone, then in this moment, that is my truth. I either move forward in what exists in the moment, or I stagnate in useless reasoning and denial. Thoughts that say, *I shouldn't feel this way,* or, *That's not nice,* or, *Being angry isn't what a spiritual person does*, are unconscious, unnecessary, and unfounded. When I believe these thoughts I deny what is true for me in the moment. This keeps me stuck, and hurting.

Questioning The Escort

The external minutiae that I try to control is inconsequential. I must tend my own backyard. I do that by flowing emotion, accepting unconditionally, and being the lucid eyewitness. I ask questions, then wait in silence for the answer to emerge independently from within. The mind must wait for the gut to answer. The questions are to be weighed in the body, not the mind.

Problems are escorts to
new levels of Consciousness.

What is this "problem" trying to tell me? Is it moving me toward a new course? Is it trying to get me to acknowledge what is true for me, and to move toward honoring that? What else is true about the situation that I'm omitting, overlooking or denying? What role am I playing in it? What can I learn? When I realize, not reason, the answers to some of these questions, the problem transforms itself, because I no longer need the problem. Problems are escorts to new levels of Consciousness.

EMPOWERMENT:
Don't shoot the messenger, everything serves. Get lucid, accept, and welcome your truths.

PROCRASTINATION

By Any Other Name

Most of us dabble in a bit of procrastination here and there. Some master it so well, that they don't notice it peeking out from behind their stories. Procrastination is tricky, versatile, and covert.

Procrastination is a cousin to resistance. It frustrates and sometimes slows us down to a stop. It may be camouflaging the fear of failure, or even the fear of success. The mind believes that the endeavor I am avoiding is just too painful, boring, difficult or frightening. Procrastination is the thinking mind's go-nowhere struggle with itself.

There is also the type of procrastination that is trying to tell me that never getting this task done is in my highest good. This is my higher Self trying to get a word in edgewise. Sometimes procrastination is telling me not to do something. In this case it would be beneficial to pass, change course, or walk away. By any other name, procrastination is a sign post. Recognizing this puts me back in the driver's seat.

Getting My Shift Together

In being honest with myself, I realize that I've been procrastinating. I accept that, completely and unconditionally. Wordlessly, I flow any emotions that may arise. I ask myself,

What is the real and honest reason that I am procrastinating? I ask this question from a place of awareness.

This is not the thinking mind's invitation for a romp through reasoning. Rather it is the prelude to making myself available for the clarity of my truth to emerge. Procrastination reveals its message when I give it my lucid attention. It's time to get my shift together.

Perhaps I recognize that I'm just burnt out. Maybe underneath it all my mind feels that I'm not competent enough for the task, or conversely, that I'm overqualified. Maybe there are distractions keeping me from moving ahead. I may recognize an uncomfortable element that I am avoiding.

If I don't know the answer in this moment, it's okay. I can, however, leave an inquiry on the back burner. The more I practice being the lucid eyewitness, freeing myself from the noise of surplus thought and postulation, the more I welcome answers, solutions and guidance to pop in.

In The Meantime

If my gut isn't completely in opposition, there are other ways to work around or through procrastination. With an open mind and no attachment, I try beginning with the desired outcome in mind. Identifying a goal, desire or plan can be the grease this wheel needs. Clear intent can go a long way.

The same holds true for other types of leverage like psyching myself up with positive self-talk. Maybe a mood board will get the juices going. Incentive may also do the trick. *If I do a little of this, I'll give myself a little of that.* Sometimes all it takes is a quick recharge. Maybe take a walk, to completely shift my focus and refresh myself. Changing gears can prompt a fresh start.

I can approach what I'm avoiding in segments. Maybe I'll move the furniture and tape up the molding today, and do the actual painting tomorrow. Or, I can ease the pain of an unsavory task by popping in some ear buds and listening to something that moves me from the inside out. If approaching a task in segments, or a transformative idea doesn't cut it, I try letting self-kindness choose. I can't go wrong with a little patience and self-kindness.

What's The Message?

The real task at hand may be learning to surrender to the universal flow, instead of to the mind's schedule.

In accepting my inner resistance, I may discover that today is just not the day for this task. Is my mind leading the way, or is my guidance? The real task at hand may be learning to surrender to the universal flow, instead of to the mind's schedule.

Getting procrastination's message may be more important than getting the task completed.

I choose to make the effort to retrain my brain to respond from lucidity, as opposed to reacting from unconsciousness. While awake, I recognize procrastination as a message, and avoid falling inadvertently into its tail-chasing stagnation. Getting procrastination's message may be more important than getting the task completed.

EMPOWERMENT:
The sign post of procrastination tells me that it's time to FUEL up, and to silently survey my own inner landscape.

REGRET

Lamenting Reality

To regret is to lament reality.

Regret is a painful story that gnaws at you little by little. To regret is to believe things should, would or could have gone differently than they had. To regret is to lament reality. Regret can be derived from things that happened, and from things that didn't happen. Pining away for a love that never blossomed, a trip never taken, a skill never learned, can be viewed through the filter of regret. Anything viewed through regret-colored glasses, feels bad. Feeling bad is a signal to take a closer look. If it hurts, there is a realization to be had.

The pain of regret is a reminder to give up the futile attempt at resisting reality. I don't have to like or agree with something to accept that it took place. Now it's over. It may have been over for thirty years, only to be kept alive in my head. Regret weighs me down.

Wishing regret on someone, or using it as a punishment, only perpetuates suffering and hinders Conscious expansion. Dropping regret does not mean that I don't care, didn't learn a lesson, or that I don't feel love or remorse.

Beyond Regret

*Regret is the fence between
me and unlimited possibility.*

Who knows what waits on the other side of the story of regret. I may say, do, or create something that changes lives for the better, individually or globally. I may educate, as to prevent future pain and suffering. I may finish something I started, find something I've been searching for, or blossom into my potential. Regret is the fence between me and unlimited possibility.

For everyone there is a path. Each path offers both pain and pleasure, both of which support our awakening. The thinking mind believes it must figure out why things happen, or why they do not happen. This is the first questionable belief. Things happen the way they do, even when the thinking mind cannot fathom a reason. This is often hard for the mind to accept. It uses reasoning and logic to formulate beliefs that say that the Universe, God, or Life has wronged it in some way.

Such a thought is painful. This tells me that my mind is having a misunderstanding. There is something it doesn't know, or isn't seeing. If in this moment I don't know why, then in this moment I don't need to know why. History reminds me that the flow of life does not depend on the thinking mind's understanding or approval.

However, the comfortable, enjoyable flow of my life does depend on acceptance. The more the mind is able to accept actuality, the smoother my life experience flows. I move on, heal, or recognize an empowerment. I keep the mind open to receiving any lesson or understanding that my resistance may have kept from me. I'm willing to accept unconditionally and in faith, that God and Life itself does unfold in the highest good of all.

Bringing myself back to a lucid state keeps me on the outside of the story. It is from the aware state of lucidity that I can look at a story without falling into it, and suffering again. Flowing the silent emotions of regret loosens my mind's grasp on it. I ask where the highest good lies, without attachment or expectation. I listen and feel for the subtle promptings of inner Guidance. In lucidity, I open myself to the inner shifts of realization, where the pain of regret is removed as an obstacle in the current of life.

EMPOWERMENT:
To regret is to lament reality. In acceptance, I remove the painful obstacle of regret and rejoin the flow of life.

RELATIONSHIPS

Bath Water

The experience of relationships, as well as "problems," both benefit from the same adage. *Don't throw out the baby with the bath water.* It behooves me to get the message from these messengers, before I part ways. If not, where ever I go, I will find them. Different places, different faces, offering me the same realizations that I missed the first time, and maybe the nineteen times after that.

If your loved one has been a source of annoyance, you are with the right person. Believe it or not, this person is one of your best teachers. My mind's theory is that the more a person irritates you, the bigger an opportunity they offer you. That's not to say that you don't experience them as pushy, uninvolved, or disapproving. I'm pointing to the opportunity of being exposed to those very things, and using them as a means of awakening into greater understanding.

It's Not You, It's Me

Awakening into greater understanding sounds great, but how does that translate into my everyday life? How do I disengage the triggers that have developed over time? If I find myself in a relationship where I'm becoming irritated, noticing the irritation is what wakes me up. As the lucid eyewitness, I notice thought and emotion that need my attention and consideration.

It's never about them.
It's always about me.

I look to myself to gain clarity. I survey my behavior and participation in a relationship. I flow emotion in unconditional acceptance, so that I don't get stuck in anger or sadness. I do the work, or I don't. I look for my truths, the ones that the thinking mind does not want to admit. The truths that are conveniently tied up with ribbons of reasoning, to get myself to believe them. Itchy little truths about self. Gaining these perspectives allows me to spot my own unconscious reactions within a relationship. It's never about them. It's always about me. It's always simple, even when it's not easy.

When something shifts on the inside,
people, places and things shift on the outside.

I have done this work. It has afforded me great realization about self and others. I have experienced people changing right before my eyes. This is not to say that we work on ourselves to change others. It is a byproduct of Conscious expansion. When something shifts on the inside, people, places and things shift on the outside.

Relationship Duality

There are two kinds of relationships. There is the direct relationship and the relationship once removed. My relationship with you is once removed by the filters of my own conjecture. My mind-made identity interacts with your mind-made identity. Unmonitored minds, bouncing around, hoping not to bump into each other.

You are everything you've been hoping for.

I have a direct connection with you when I offer you my full and wordless attention. Lucidity comes with no judgements or expectations. Just the real me, seeing the real you. This is an authentic relationship. Authenticity enhances our encounters, and evolves our relationships to new and deeper levels. You see someone you've known for years, for the very first time. Authentic living makes for authentic relationships. You are everything you've been hoping for.

EMPOWERMENT:
My relationships are once removed by the filter of thoughts and beliefs. Authentic living makes for authentic relationships, with self and others.

RESISTANCE

Anti-Reality

Resistance is the stealthy shapeshifter of unconsciousness. Its clever anti-reality disguises include anger, hate, addiction, and regret. Sometimes we see it, sometimes we don't. We are in resistance far more than we realize. *I won't let that happen... I don't like what so-and-so is saying... This shouldn't be like that... No, no, and no way.* Resistance is to disapprove or dispute reality.

> *Unawareness is tainted with the automatic reaction of resistance.*

I live in resistance when I push away from being wrong, or making a mistake. I live in resistance when I oppose the isness of the moment. Resistance puts me in a state of limited possibility. Unawareness is tainted with the automatic reaction of resistance.

Manifesting Mojo

My manifesting mojo is my vibe. When I'm in resistance, I'm emitting a feel-bad vibe. The stuff that matches that vibe is what manifests into my life. When I use my focus and energy to protest reality, I produce my own discomfort, and that discomfort produces even more like experiences.

My vibe broadcasts 24/7. The last thing I want is to be unknowingly lost in thought, while my vibe is requesting more pain and suffering. As the lucid eyewitness, flowing unconditionally, I can make kinder choices for myself and stream a much higher vibe.

The Lie Of Resistance

The mind's reasoning for resistance is to uphold what it believes, and to push away what it does not want. Most of the mind's beliefs go unexamined. In addition, the thinking mind really has no way of being 100% sure what is in my best interest. The mind believes that some reality is just too tough to deal with. Like a loss of some kind, or something that changes your identity as you know it. Some truth does feel excruciating, when it is resisted.

> *Unconditional acceptance is*
> *the arch enemy of resistance.*

Acceptance only stings for the first few moments. After that, I'm either free, or well on my way. Unconditional acceptance is the arch enemy of resistance. It washes resistance away, along with its symptoms, discomfort and stagnation.

*When I spare myself the effort of
resistance, I am free to use that effort
where it would be most beneficial.*

Emotions flow, swell, and heal. They don't kill. I have experienced issues that I could only glance at, until the day came that I could stare it down and watch it melt. When I spare myself the effort of resistance, I am free to use that effort where it would be most beneficial. When I embrace the isness of my situation, I set myself free.

EMPOWERMENT:
Unconditional acceptance eradicates the obstacle and discomfort of resistance, opening my door to limitless possibility.

SADNESS

The Fallacy Of Loss

Sadness takes me out of a positive, thriving state. I can't stay out there for too long before I begin to wither. The recognition that my life is my responsibility, allows me to do what it takes to step out of a painful misunderstanding, by seeing through to the truth.

The story of loss, and the love
that I have are two separate things.

We feel sad when we believe we have lost something. If I love you more than words can say, but you are no longer here with me, that has nothing to do with the ever-present, everlasting, unconditional love that I have for you. As the eyewitness to thought, I recognize that fully associating my attention on the story of loss, is where sadness is created and experienced. The story of loss, and the love that I have are two separate things.

True love and joy is part of That which we are, and cannot be derived or housed outside of ourselves. Outside of my story of sadness lies reality, where I am awake and aware. In awareness, I connect with Self, and rejoice in love. In doing so, I have not lost you. I am always connected to you.

Sadness can also be experienced when we believe we have taken a blow to, or lost part of our identity. We are not our identity. Who we really are is already whole and complete. The experience of sadness is to forget who I am. Luckily, the pain of sadness comes to alert us to our momentary unconsciousness.

Mind And Body

Realizing the difference between Self and my story of sadness does not imply that the physical emotion of sadness should be ignored or denied. The physical moves a lot slower than the nonphysical, and should not be forgotten or suppressed.

*Honoring painful emotions frees the body
from the ill effects of their negative energy.*

I may experience a mentally freeing realization that changes my experience immediately, and still have some residual emotions of sadness. In applying my silent attention on the body, I may notice tightened muscles begin to release, or I may feel the need to wordlessly cry for a moment. Emotion knows the way. Your only job is to witness it. Allow emotion to emerge, peak and dissipate, without mental evaluation. Honoring painful emotions frees the body from the ill effects of their negative energy.

The Whole Truth And Nothing But

Anything that does not feel good is derived from my mind's account of the event. While it may be true that so-and-so did such-and-such, even purposefully knowing that it could hurt me, I no longer accept just that scenario. Why would I? There's nothing good in it for me. There must be something more that I'm overlooking.

What role does my thinking mind play in this situation? I slow down and zoom out to mentally witness the event. I am willing to recognize my truths. Am I unnecessarily taking things personally? Have I assumed incorrectly, or unwittingly imposed myself in some way? Maybe I forgot to look for the gifts that the situation offers. Have I taken into account that this is a benevolent construct, and that everything happens to increase my degree of Consciousness?

The Degree Of Consciousness

Only in my own unconsciousness can someone's fearful or angry actions hurt me.

Only in my own unconsciousness can someone's fearful or angry actions hurt me. I'd have to join them in their unconsciousness for me to feel sadness and suffer. FUELing my life supports me in gaining clarity of the bigger picture. When I see the bigger picture, I no longer see any truth to my sadness, and it begins to fade away.

> *I cannot treat you any greater than my*
> *degree of Consciousness in the moment.*

We all sleepwalk, no matter how much we may love one another. We are all the same in that when we stand in the circle of our own unconsciousness, we are unable to accept, love and support unconditionally. In our unawareness we believe that someone or something should be different than they are in the moment. We do the best we can, with what we have, from where we are. I cannot treat you any greater than my degree of Consciousness in the moment. This is the human condition. *Forgive them, for they know not what they do.* When I am unconscious, submersed in unexamined, unnecessary thought, I know not what I do.

Apples And Oranges

If I know someone wanting and willing to better a situation through awareness, I do what it takes to support them. I reciprocate the effort by making it a point to stay awake with them. We both make an effort, and before long old programming begins to change. Sadness fades and we begin to experience each other in new and wonderful ways.

> *When I fall into unconsciousness,*
> *pain and suffering are inevitable.*

My job is to stay awake, and to accept the isness of the moment, recognizing the mirror and opportunities that life offers. When I am the lucid eyewitness, awake and aware, I can do that. When I fall into unconsciousness, pain and suffering are inevitable.

When the fruit is ripe, it falls from the tree.

If someone makes it clear, whether by words or by repeated actions, that they choose not to make the effort to step into awareness, I make the effort to accept that. I act in self-love and remove myself from their path. This means nothing but that everyone is awakening in their own time. We are all where we are supposed to be. I respect their decision to not make the effort, and wish them well. They are not ready. They just don't have it in them in the moment. Perhaps another day. Apples or oranges, it's all good. It's never personal. When the fruit is ripe, it falls from the tree.

Ripe It Up

If I don't choose for me, then sadness is not my biggest misunderstanding.

When I choose *for* me, I choose what is kind. I choose to be the lucid eyewitness. I choose to flow with life in unconditional acceptance. I make the effort to rise up out of sadness. If I don't choose *for* me, then sadness is not my biggest misunderstanding.

If I can't just jump out of sadness, I will lovingly ask myself to come up with one feel-good thought. Even during the times that I'd prefer to wallow in my torment, making the effort to count my blessings, or to visualize feel-good desires, slows down the ship-of-doom, and turns it around. It takes considerably less effort to see through my sad story from a feel-good place.

EMPOWERMENT:
Only in unawareness can I experience sadness. I awaken from the story and reconnect to my power. I choose *for* me.

SCARCITY

Recognize And Redirect

If I consistently place the power of my focus on lack, I shouldn't wonder why the experience of abundance eludes me. The more I look at life through the notion of scarcity, the more scarcity I experience in my life. The problem is that I don't notice when I'm looking at life through my scarcity-colored glasses.

Witnessing thought affords me the possibility to change my life experience. I may be unwittingly practicing saving the best for last, or taking or using less than I really want. Every time I catch a thought that says, "There's never enough" or "This won't last," I wake up to catch the scarcity programming in action.

If it seems that scarcity is everywhere I look, and I can't help but look at it, that does not mean that I must place the power of my attention on it, or believe in it. Ideally, I would not resist it, nor would I focus on it. Instead, I remind myself that my worth and potential are not derived from or dependent on my surroundings. Positive thinking, gratitude, questioning thought, and lucidity, are some of the tweaks that change the programming.

The Good Towels

We have a joke around here about a few household items. You know the ones, the "good" towels, the "good" candles, tablecloth, soaps, etc. All the good stuff that I'm saving incase the Pope comes by. This too is a scarcity mentality, even if it is in the name of papal preparedness.

The trick is to see it, not just say it.

The experience of scarcity has the potential to be painful. Especially for those of us in a survival mode. Luckily, this place of duality offers another side to every coin. If I believe scarcity is true for me, then abundance would have to be true for me as well. The trick is to see it, not just say it. Stay on alert to notice all the plentifulness and abundances in life.

Seeing Through Scarcity

Awakening is about thought noticing itself in action.

This is really not about how much or how little of anything I have. It's really a retraining. Awakening is about thought noticing itself in action. Being awake is to recognize painful thoughts and habits. I'm not trying to eliminate pain, as pain serves its purpose by waking me up. I'm trying to eliminate the misconception that causes the pain.

Changing The Signal

It is the vibe emitted from the emotion of scarcity, that broadcasts a signal to the Universe that says I want more of that. More of what matches that vibe. More scarcity, in its many forms.

There's a big disparity between talking about how great abundance would feel, and really noticing it in my life. Noticing abundance is to go beyond the words, into what abundance feels like. Now I'm broadcasting a signal that tells the Universe to manifest more of that, more abundance.

Each time I use the old, ugly thing so that I don't wear out the new shiny thing, I broadcast scarcity. While I may work to eradicate scarcity in my life, doing things like this unintentionally creates more of it.

Each time I see my loved ones and allow myself to recognize all the love there is, I broadcast abundance. When I count my many blessings and feel grateful, I broadcast abundance. When I give freely of things, time and my attention, I broadcast abundance.

EMPOWERMENT:
What I see is what I get.

SHAME

The Ubiquitous Misconception

Shame is a painful story that cuts deeper than most. The story of shame treads on a thinking mind's most sacred ground, its personal identity. There are as many things that I can be ashamed of, as my mind can conjure up in its imagination. I may be ashamed of something I do, something I did, where I come from, what I look like, what I don't do, and what I may or may not have. In the unmonitored mind, shame is a ubiquitous misconception.

Shame says that I am flawed. There's something not right, not up to par, broken, or unacceptable about me. The real me, outside of the mind-made identity, is Consciousness. Consciousness couldn't possibly be flawed. When I believe unnoticed, unexamined misconceptions, I believe the illusion and I suffer. Shame, and the reasoning it rode in on, are mind-made misconceptions.

Imposing And Opposing

The pain of shame is fed by my resistance to it. I resist the story as well as the messenger of anguish, who have come to help me to awaken. Resistance is a demanding obstacle. It requires me to live in avoidance of the shame. I am held captive within this painful habit.

*When the mind stops imposing its opinions,
and opposing reality, I am able to move forward.*

Free will says that I can choose what is self-kind and accept where I am, or I can resist and agonize. Shame begins to vanish in the presence of self-kindness. When the mind stops imposing its opinions, and opposing reality, I am able to move forward.

Damaging Deterrents

Society tells us that we should feel ashamed for having done a horrible thing. "Shame on you." Saying that to someone is not helpful, but in unawareness that's the best we've got. It is a misguided attempt at preventing you from repeating your dishonorable behavior. How likely is it that I will act better if I feel worse about myself? Clarity frees us from inflicting pain on ourselves or others.

Reboot

Shame often feeds addictive behaviors. The more the mind believes it has something to be ashamed of, the more it reaches outside of itself for the thing it uses to help keep those feelings at bay. This habit reinforces the faulty programming that keeps us moving around in a painful circle.

There are some of us that feel they can't even look at what they feel ashamed of, much less accept or rise above it. Just for one moment, imagine what it would be like if you could look directly at what you feel ashamed of. Imagine if you were one of those people that just said, *This thing right here has caused me so much pain, and now I'm working on accepting it, fixing it, or healing it.* What if you yanked open the door, grabbed the most despised skeleton in the closet, and waved it around in all its actual isness? This is it. This is what I'm so ashamed of.

You will realize that the skeleton is not what has been holding you captive, rather the fear-based resistance is. Fear of what other's may think, or how things will change. This can feel like the end of the world. Maybe it is. The end of a world where you unnecessarily live life trying to sidestep fear.

I'm not saying that you have to parade your skeletons, fears and misunderstandings down Main Street. We're not obligated to broadcast the inner work we do. We may be afraid of what other's will think, but it's really about what we think. We are greater than our stories. We are greater than our fears. We make mistakes and have misunderstandings. The first step to freedom is in the privacy of our own head. So the mind has faulty programming, and we have the power to change it.

The *Do Not Enter* Exit

> ***There is no absolute truth in***
> ***what fear whispers, because I live in***
> ***a construct where anything is possible.***

As the eyewitness, I begin to catch the thoughts that speak of shame. I notice the internal whispering that says I'm not good enough as I am. I notice the sudden flutter of feel-bad unfurl, as I try to get through the day. Noticing these painful thoughts gives me the chance to grab them by the toe, and drag them out into the light. There is no absolute truth in what fear whispers, because I live in a construct where anything is possible.

I sit silently, holding the wordless space for unconditional acceptance to rise up and set me free. Unconditional acceptance of myself and my life, just as it happens to be in the moment. I desensitize shame, by looking directly at it, and allowing the blockade of unprocessed emotion to flow and go. I do these things certainly not because of what anyone else may think. I do it because it hurts too much not to. This is my responsibility. I rise to the occasion, in my own time. This is between me, and myself.

Shame hides behind a door marked, "Do Not Enter." Despite the lies that shame would tell, we are so worth the effort. When we march past fear, and kick down that door, we find the way out. The way out is through. Use your power for good.

EMPOWERMENT:

I choose to witness thought, flow emotion, and exercise lucidity in unconditional acceptance. These are the self-loving practices that free me from the illusionary prison of shame.

STRESS

Not What, How

Stress is the internal commotion that I feel when my mind is splashing around in unmonitored, feel-bad thinking. It is a frivolous expenditure of focus and energy. If I do this long and often enough, I create a new habit. A habit made to be broken.

It's not about what I'm doing, it's always about how I'm doing it. Am I on or off? Am I awake and aware, or am I totally consumed by thought? Is my thinking mind rambling incessantly about half empty glasses and never enough time?

Sometimes there really isn't enough time to get it all done. Things don't go as planned, they break, or don't arrive on time. That's just the isness of it. I am no longer interested in sabotaging health and efficacy, by falling unconscious into painful, stress-producing stories.

Crawling across the finish line means I did it wrong. It means there's a better way, and if others can find it, so can I. Life is hard enough without my thinking mind cutting me down at the knees in the face of seeming chaos. Unmonitored, negative thinking, even unwittingly, is the equivalent to shooting myself in the foot on an uphill climb. I'd rather not.

The Hierarchy

I remind myself of the hierarchy. The higher Self is the CEO of this life experience. It is whole and complete, and knows the itinerary. It's forthcoming in directing the way toward what is in my best interest, and what serves my awakening.

The thinking mind, however immeasurably perceptive, is the President, in charge of Production. The mind is a tool for Self. When the mind disconnects from Self, it disconnects from its own inner compass. The inevitable, unmanaged mental commotion, is what interferes with the mind's ability to reconnect.

Flipping The Coin

All the stress in the world couldn't add more hours to the day, or extend my deadlines. Stress sucks the enjoyment out of life, and renders me less likely to gain headway. Not to mention the negative physical effects it has on the body.

> *No matter what is happening outside*
> *of me, I have the power to respond,*
> *rather than react out of stress.*

Getting stressed is a red flag alerting me that I have fallen unconscious into thought. When feeling super-stressed, I give myself a minute to slow down to a stop, take a breath and bring myself back to lucidity. The internal, perpetual calm is located right outside of the continual mental evaluation. It is the still space that whispers that everything will work itself out if I follow what feels good, and what feels kind. No matter what is happening outside of me, I have the power to respond, rather than react out of stress.

> *My balanced well-being is in my highest good, and in the highest good of all.*

Unconditional acceptance obliterates what stands in my way. My balanced well-being is in my highest good, and in the highest good of all. It's much kinder to come into the present moment and tap into higher intelligence, than it is to endure the pessimistic opposition of the thinking mind.

Living outside of the ongoing mental dictate is a much more enjoyable experience than being stressed, and it yields much better results. To keep myself in the zone, I make the effort to balance thinking with being. The four living meditation practices of FUEL Your Life are the tools that I pull out of my pocket when the heat is on and the pressure is high. It only takes a couple of moments to acknowledge and flow some emotion. I accept that in this moment I'm feeling pressured. I shift into being the eyewitness, recognizing the thoughts that are turning up the heat. Staying lucid keeps me from falling back into panic mode.

If I stay out of the thought-storm that's producing the feeling of stress, I start feeling better in minutes. I have noticed my shoulders come down from, unknowingly, having been up around my neck. I recognize all the gritting and taut muscles, as they start to release into the peace of a quiet mind. I have the power do these things anywhere, even if it is just for a few seconds. I can do them in the midst of disruption, while stuck in traffic, and even in the boardroom.

When I witness the mind's activity, I notice the quality of my thoughts, and make the necessary adjustments. Deleting, and updating thought changes and enhances my life experiences. The quieter the mind, the greater the connection to inner peace.

I may be only one deep breath away from being escorted into the present moment, of peace and limitless possibility.

The more that I practice these efforts, especially in the heat of the moment, the easier they become. I may be only one deep breath away from being escorted into the present moment, of peace and limitless possibility. Making these small efforts, is the difference between crawling across the finish line, and dancing over it.

EMPOWERMENT:
Stress is a cue to use my tools, and to allow it to be easy. My balanced well-being is in the highest good of all.

STUCK

Beating Dead Beliefs

Feeling stuck? Stuck in a rut, an unfulfilling job, a relationship? Maybe you feel like you're stuck in your own life. We work hard to better our lives, to create change that just doesn't manifest. We have the dreaded experience of running in place.

In witnessing thought, I have discovered a belief that does not serve me. My mind reasons that if I make an effort, it's only right, it's only fair, that I should see some type of positive gain or change. When it does not pan out, this belief becomes my mind's argument with reality. The mind's arguments and misbeliefs are my pain and stagnation. So how do I get unstuck?

Logic doesn't always equal truth, and
reasoning never trumps inner guidance.

Our elders meant well when they taught us that hard work brings favorable results. Not that there's anything wrong with hard work. If you want change that is in your highest good, hard work must be presence-based or inspired, not fear-based, or reason-based. What's the point of exhausting myself to set sail, if I'm traveling in the wrong direction? Logic doesn't always equal truth, and reasoning never trumps inner guidance.

Tail Chasing

When I mix unsupervised reasoning with conflicting beliefs, I have the recipe for chasing my tail.

    There have been many times that I contorted myself trying to move ahead. The meticulous mind examined all possibility, except for its own approach and avoidance tactics. This is where I would work hard to create something that would be thwarted by my underlying, hidden beliefs to the contrary. When I mix unsupervised reasoning with conflicting beliefs, I have the recipe for chasing my tail.

    I may have been working hard, but the only movement I made was in a circle. To a thinking mind, this is an invitation for additional stories about insufficient luck, victimization, failure, and disappointment. The mind is not as interested in the content of its thinking, as much as it is interested in the act of thinking. Life is much easier when I witness and evaluate the chatter of the mind, instead of just believing everything it says.

Even if I change my job, residence, relationships, or my looks, old beliefs will supersede my efforts.

When I don't notice the mind's actions, I can't understand why I seem so stuck. The mind is repeatedly exercising the same beliefs, performing the same acts, and expecting different results. Even if I change my job, home, relationships, or my looks, old beliefs will supersede my efforts.

Getting Unstuck

While I was trying to move stuff outside of myself, the stuff outside of myself was trying to make something move on the inside. Things not working out the way the mind thinks they should, would or could, despite my exhausting efforts, isn't bad luck or punishment. It is an invitation. It is an invitation to use my innate tools, and to take an honest look at myself and uphold my truths. I want to know if I've been chasing the wrong things, and not giving the right things a chance to find me.

Unconditional acceptance of the situation is the first step at unsticking myself from the story of being stuck. As the eyewitness to thought, I save my own sweat and sanity by noticing the mind beating dead and unfounded beliefs. I must let go of what the mind grasps at, and make friends with the unknown.

These perspectives produced a powerful lesson. It doesn't matter how driven or dedicated I am, if I am pushing in the wrong direction. My first and most important responsibility is to be awake and aware in the moment. Tuned in to my own Guidance, and free from indiscriminate, untrue beliefs.

The mind simply never knows for sure. That's the point, it doesn't have to know. Instead of wandering aimlessly through life, experiencing one blind attempt after another, I'm opting for a better way. I made friends with both, not knowing, and the experience of being stuck. I accepted being at a standstill, and I stood still. I relinquished the needy grasp on forcing change. Things began to move when I stopped forcing them to move. I stayed awake and kept an eye and ear open for the promptings, inclinations and penchants of inner guidance.

Inner guidance comes as happy or lucky coincidences. It manifests as urges or sudden inspiration. The key is to trust it, and indulge yourself without letting the mind reason it away. I learned that the things that seemed illogical or frivolous, turned out to be joyful and fruitful. I learned to get out of my own way by ripping the reins right out of the thinking mind's little ego-loving hands, and blindly going with my flow.

As the eyewitness to the inner activity of thought and emotion, we recognize what feeds the experience of being stuck. Is the mind constantly engaged in its storytelling, or is the mind quiet, open and using its tools? I empower and free myself by accepting the situation, examining thought, flowing emotion, and following the map of my own joy. This translates to bulldozing the way out, and enjoying the smooth flow of life again.

EMPOWERMENT:
I am never so stuck that I cannot reconnect with my power, by surrendering to my own Guidance.

SUCCESS

The Semblance Of Success

One of the ways we measure success is by the accumulation of money and things. While we may possess many things, and maintain a large bank account, we may be internally bankrupt.

In unawareness we mistakenly
measure our self-worth by the scale
of material and monetary attainment.

In unawareness, I believe that part of who I am is linked to something outside of myself. When I no longer have the possessions of success, the mind considers it a diminishing of self, and I suffer. Unawakened success is superficial, intermittent, or temporary at best. In unawareness we mistakenly measure our self-worth by the scale of material and monetary attainment.

Awakened success is enjoyed when we realize that who we are is not a result of things acquired. How do I know when I have fallen asleep in success? When I become attached. When I see or consider someone or something as an attribute or component of who I am.

Once the feeling of need begins to dictate my actions and decisions, I find the fear of losing what I have and the fear of not having enough. I've fallen asleep. The moment I recognize my attachment, is the moment that I awaken. It is in awareness that I fully and authentically enjoy the toys of outer success.

Authentic Success

Authentic success is not about doing better than the next guy, or better than yesterday. It's not all about determination, or being the most driven. What then is true success?

> ***True success is connecting to Self.***

Waking up to the present moment, devoid of the surfeit of unneeded thought, is a lucid moment. In a lucid moment, I connect with my authentic Self, the real me outside of the mind-made identity. We come to experience this connection as benevolence, abundance and joy. It is your birthright to have an authentically wonderful life experience, ever-changing, always joyful. True success is connecting to Self.

Authentic success is enjoying a direct experience to the people, places and things in our life, without the veil of learned, repetitive thought. It is to fly without a net, and soar. It is to meet and revel in who you really are. Real success is to be awake in the dream. The dynamic of authentic success is how you bring Consciousness into this world. This has also been described as living your life purpose, or the life or your dreams.

Authentic living is the ultimate success.

Real success is the discovery of our own greatness, and the resulting joys of authentic living. None of which is dependent on external acquisition. We may thoroughly enjoy abundance of all things, without the pitfalls of attachment or the misbeliefs of self-worth. Authentic living is the ultimate success.

She Who Dares

Climb out on the limb. That is where the fruit is. The worst thing that can happen is that you fall. So you get up, and climb back up there. In the end, it doesn't matter how much fruit, or how many falls you have had. For she who dares, wins.

EMPOWERMENT:
True success is awakening into the bliss of an authentic life experience.

SURRENDER

Beyond The Misunderstanding

I used to think surrender meant giving up. The connotation reeked of failure. Surrendering to anything felt like backing down, or caving in. My thinking mind considered surrender a dirty word, while my drive and commitment ate surrender for breakfast. Well, that's before I understood what it really meant.

Surrender can be described as unconditional acceptance. Logically understanding the definition of surrender allows us to get a foot in the door of really knowing surrender, and the empowerment it offers. It is in going beyond the words into the experience of surrender, that allows us to walk through that door, into the flow of our highest good.

Surrender is the falling
away of what is unnecessary.

Beyond the concept, what does the experience of surrender feel like? It is a release. The experience of surrender feels wonderful because we are letting go of what we do not need. Surrender is the falling away of what is unnecessary. Spiritual growth is a lessening, not an adding to. We drop what feels bad. We release what is not required in the moment. We surrender trying to control, or hold on. Internally, we let go.

Holy Shift

The thinking mind isn't always a team player. It doesn't always take direction well, even if higher intelligence is pointing the way. The mind likes to make the plan, call the shots, say what, and make its own rules. That's a lot of work, and most often, that's exactly what it ends up feeling like.

In surrendering resistance, I shift into the space of serendipity and divine providence.

Surrender is off-loading the to-do list. We get to drop worry and fear-based action, in exchange for the peaceful power of a lucid moment. In surrendering resistance, I shift into the space of serendipity and divine providence. When we're plugged in, watching for sign posts, and listening for direction, life flows easily and enjoyably.

Theres a difference between going after something, and something coming to me. Surrendering into unconditional acceptance is what bridges that gap. I practice surrendering my thinking mind's desire to constantly control it all, even in so much as an approval or disapproval. I pay attention to new interests, or inspiration, and indulge myself. When the gut overrides the thinking, life begins falling into our lap.

Release And Relax

Reasoning does not equal truth.

What feels bad is the mind's desire to deny, change, fix or push away the reality of the moment. It uses reasoning to uphold and enforce its opinions and actions. The mind is doing the best that it can. Although as thorough as reasoning can be, inherently it's still just a shot in the dark. Reasoning does not equal truth.

Surrender does not mean to give up, or to allow someone or something to devour us. It is an internal release of resistance. This empowers us in two ways. First, We immediately reap peace and relief. As if that's not reason enough, and self-love says that it is, we also disengage the mirror of resistance. Surrender opens the door to inspired action and authentic change.

When I say that I surrender to the isness of the moment, but internally I am really still in resistance, life will mirror that resistance back to me. When I am able to fully surrender internally, I allow life to cradle me. I drop the boulders of opposition and am hands-free to move on, move up and make positive change.

*Surrender stands between
me and inspired action.*

There's a disparity between action, and inspired action. Action comes from the thinking mind and feels like work. Inspired action comes from the higher Self and feels like drive, passion or fun, even if it is hard work. Surrender stands between me and inspired action. Surrender fear and resistance for the bliss of an authentic experience.

EMPOWERMENT:
In surrender, I allow life to support me in the divine providence of what is.

VULNERABILITY

Shields Down

Vulnerability, in its true untainted form, is empowering, invigorating, and excruciatingly uncomfortable. It is a thing we have come to avoid at all costs. We have developed an automatic reaction to sidestepping vulnerability, and in turn forfeit its secret stores. Without being willing to be vulnerable, authentic change will wait just outside of my reach.

To be vulnerable is to greet life, shields down, in unconditional acceptance of what is. This can be frightening to a thinking mind. It's feels like I'm lowering my defenses, and hoping that something won't pop up to try to shame, blame or wrong me to death.

Being vulnerable is to drop all conditioned reactions, and allow to the real me to spontaneously respond in an authentic way.

Being vulnerable is to drop all conditioned reactions, and to allow the real me to spontaneously respond in an authentic way. It feels risky because it is a relinquishment of the mind's usual attempt at defense and control. This invites fear-based thought. *What if things don't go the way I think they should? What if I seem unpleasant, ungrateful or unlikable?*

Stepping out from behind the mind's defensive shield of evaluating, labeling, judging, and contemplating, has that naked-in-public feeling. When I first tried stepping out from behind my mind's protective shield, it felt like trying not to flinch when someone was pretending to smack me. That's only because a defensive shield is a hard-wired habit, not because it cannot be disengaged.

As difficult as it may seem, allowing myself to be vulnerable is the biggest investment in self that I can make. Moreover, once I experienced the awesome return on investment, my thinking mind was much more willing to enter into the shields-down mode.

Open The Gate

The more I resist being vulnerable, the more I perpetuate my own discomfort and stagnation. It is within a vulnerable moment that I recognize the mind's misapprehensions and fears, because the mind is not busy deflecting and rejecting. These realizations are the difference between spiritual understanding and actual, authentic spiritual growth. It is the difference between being stagnated and soaring free.

> *Vulnerability is the gateway to an*
> *authentic life experience. An authentic*
> *life experience is the life of my dreams.*

My mind started to think that vulnerability may have gotten a bad rap. It may be one of those words that only sound dirty or dangerous, but really isn't. Vulnerability is the gateway to an authentic life experience. An authentic life experience is the life of my dreams.

Out Of The Box

I used to think the term, *to think outside the box*, meant to think in a creative way. I've since come to understand that it is a scientific term that means to step outside of my reactive, learned behavior, and into the space of a new response. The space outside the box is located just outside the periphery of my comfort zone. This is the space in which I feel vulnerable, the space of unbound potential.

Being in a position where anything can happen, and you're wide open to it, can be a fearful position for a thinking mind. This is the dreaded space of the unknown. A place where I can fail, be wrong, rejected or misunderstood. Fear prevents us from stepping into vulnerability. Fear stands guard around the box, bullying us to stay inside.

We inevitably feel the pangs of curtailed growth, striving but never arriving. If everything serves my awakening, how could being mistaken or "failing" be a negative thing? It's not possible. To be vulnerable is to lay down my defenses. I trade the momentary sting of recognizing fear and untruths, for authenticity, freedom and joy.

Whatever I can do in the moment is the perfect amount. If I can move outside of my comfort zone only one toe at a time, then so be it. I'll go inch by inch, second by second if I have to, until I can stay out there longer and longer.

As the eyewitness to thought and feeling, I'm free to step out of the same reactions and results, into new possibilities. In flowing the emotions that arise, I am washing away the confines of my history. Unconditional acceptance and lucidity, allow me to go with the empowering flow of vulnerability.

EMPOWERMENT:
The fast track to authentic living and spiritual growth is vulnerability.

WORRY

Off And Running

Worry is self-sabotage.

To worry is to let the thinking mind marinate in negative scenarios, depicting potential negative outcomes. Worry is unbridled, unfounded fear in action. It is an invitation for the experience of stress and anxiety. Worry is self-sabotage. Worrying is not about being silly or unproductive, it's about being unconscious. When my thinking mind is in the "off" position, I can fall victim to the feel-bad experience of worry.

Worried Sick

The distress of worry is a heads-up, that's trying to alert me to my own unawareness. Until I wake up to my unnecessary thinking, I'm doomed to stew in it. When I fall submersed into these distressing thoughts, the brain releases hormones into the bloodstream. These hormones produce feel-bad feelings, that have serious unfavorable potential, especially when let loose on the body on a regular basis. Besides feeling bad, I have now created the recipe for making my body ill. The old adage of worrying myself sick seems to be literal.

What's worse is that there is nothing that I can do about it, if I don't realize that I'm doing it. Some of us have become proficient at worry. We undermine our productive efforts by cultivating worry as a bad habit. Yielding to the habit of worry feeds nothing but the mind's gratuitous desire to splash around in thought, and the consequential anguish it creates.

New Tricks

It's time for some new tricks. If you have a pet, the teacher awaits. If not, take a look at animals in their natural environment. Animals are not plagued with being submersed in faulty and unrestrained thought, so they don't sweat the small stuff. They don't worry about how much kibble they ate, or if their rumps look fat in their fur. The only tail-chasing they do is for fun.

Animals enjoy a more direct experience with life, and so have greater access to their innate abilities. They have peace, and the contentment of unconditional acceptance. This beats the hec out of living within the confines of a bad habit. We are sometimes so submersed in unbridled thought, that we end up living life indirectly, through the veil of worry.

Quit It

Fortunately, the wheel spins in both directions. What I learn, I can unlearn. Take an honest look at it. Are you a continual worrier? Do you perpetually fall into a mental anticipation of negative scenarios? If so, this is your opportunity to wake up to worry, and to move forward on your way to freedom.

On the heels of witnessing a worrisome thought, I hold a wordless space for any momentary emotion that wants to emerge. I make the effort to resist the call of this tormenting habit, because I know there is no absolute truth in worry. It's just fearful supposition. Even if I only resist for a few moments, those moments help to weaken the strong hold of this deleterious programming.

Staying lucid, removed from the internal banter, keeps me out of worry and its detriments. It also allows me to examine thought from a safe place, and to recognize the futility of worry. Apart from having a crystal ball, I really have no way of knowing if that which I'm worrying about will ever come to fruition.

Trade the distress of worry
for the peace of acceptance, and the
optimistic excitement of the unknown.

When I experience acceptance, worry is replaced with peace. I accept that everything happens to assist my growth, and choose to stay awake for any empowerments that the Universe offers. I remind myself that I attract what I put my focus on. So if my mind is going to romp through unneeded thought, I could at least make sure that it is positive thought. I am much more effective, not to mention healthy, from an awakened, lucid state of being. Trade the distress of worry for the peace of acceptance, and the optimistic excitement of the unknown.

Making these small efforts to awaken to and break the habit of worry, cost nothing but a little bit of time. Making these efforts, is making a big investment in your mental, emotional and physical well-being. One day you will notice how much you just don't worry anymore. No new story, or willpower, you just notice how different you are. Good different. Easy and flowing. This is authentic change.

EMPOWERMENT:
Worry not, for Guidance is always there, pointing me toward my highest good.

WORTH

Meanwhile

When we are born, we are innately our true Selves. Along the way, the more we add to the mind-made identity, and the contents of the thinking mind, the more that innate connection fades. Truth becomes skewed by false beliefs, misjudgment, and illusion. It is as if we are let loose in this world to feel our way back to our true Selves. The human adventure is finding our way back. A journey, to remember what the soul already knows.

*Worth is a measuring stick
in a world of make-believe.*

Worth is a mind-made concept. It is a label, a description, an evaluation, a story formulated by the thinking mind. Worth is a measuring stick in a world of make-believe. Although the mind places worth on almost everything it thinks about or encounters, the greatest evaluation of worth is regarding self. The mind creates an identity, and then sets out on a lifelong undertaking of determining and increasing its worth.

We're out there trying to prove to ourselves, through our efforts and through the eyes of others, that we are honorable, reputable, powerful and virtuous. Underneath we grapple with merit, inferiority, and entitlement. Meanwhile, who I really am, my higher Self, my Soul, Consciousness, is already perfect. In that, there is no question of worth. Yet, the concept of worth can be a powerful asset for our tool, the thinking mind. Building self-worth is the thinking mind's work. It strengthens the connection to Self.

Living Beliefs

If I believe that I'm not worthy, I think, feel and act in ways that support that belief. The reflection of that belief, in the people and events of my life, continually offer me the opportunity to wake up to myself. Until I awaken into the misconception of unworthiness, I suffer.

Worth is a self-fulfilling prophecy.

When I fail to uphold my truths, life mirrors back the experience of being disregarded or disrespected in some way, but the thinking mind misinterprets that. Instead, I take everything personally and lay blame on external people and circumstances. I react with anger and sadness, and yield to the need to please, appease and overachieve. Worth is a self-fulfilling prophecy.

Measuring The Measuring Stick

*Self-worth is the mind's fuel
for the journey back to Self.*

It is very difficult to hide low self-worth. I may seem pleasant enough, but the space in between my words would be filled with the sent of self-loathing. I may have an impeccable record, but in the end what stands out the most is how I try too hard. Self-worth is the mind's fuel for the journey back to Self. It's one thing to say that I'm worthy, it's a completely different thing to believe it, and it's a whole new world to know it.

*The mind prompts us to avoid what feels
bad, sometimes at all costs. The problem is,
avoiding what feels bad, is costing us everything.*

Vulnerability is the gateway to authentic living. Venturing out into the transparency of vulnerability with little to no self-worth, is almost unbearable. The mind prompts us to avoid what feels bad, sometimes at all costs. The problem is, avoiding what feels bad, is costing us everything.

Do I rest when I'm tired? Do I encourage myself or beat myself up when something doesn't go the way the thinking mind thinks it should? Do I make an effort to notice my thoughts and question them? Do I give myself the gift of processing emotion or facing some of my fears? Do I include myself when I care for, nurture, comfort and love others? If the answer is no to even one of these questions, then I am not choosing *for* me. Why not? When my happiness, health and comfort are not enough leverage to inspire and motivate me to act in my highest good, I must look at self-worth.

Awakening Worth

In reality, worth is not a determining factor. My state of being is.

Positive self-worth can be achieved in two ways. We can work to create a new belief, or we can awaken. Awakening is to experience the realization of the separation of thought and Self, where the mind understands that worth has never been a question. No matter who we are, we are able to enjoy the bliss of an authentic life experience. In reality, worth is not a determining factor. My state of being is.

Healthy self-worth is also a byproduct. While practicing to FUEL my life, I was freeing myself from painful untruths, and learning how to swim with my own current. In addition, the more I made the effort to stay awake, honor my truths, and live authentically, the more self-gratitude, self-appreciation, and self-pride I experienced. While my consciousness expanded, the thinking mind was reprogramming.

I witnessed new thoughts pop up, accompanied by good feelings. *I'm so happy and grateful that I made the effort for myself. I'm so proud of myself.*

What's It Worth?

*Satisfying the longing to be good
to yourself, sparks the realization
that bliss is found in self-love.*

Beyond mental desires, there are longings. Some are big, some are small. A longing is a message from the soul. Put the world on pause and make that glorious, deep-seated connection with your longings. Go eye-to-eye with yourself in mental silence. Satisfying the longing to be good to yourself, sparks the realization that bliss is found in self-love. It's worth the effort. It's worth everything.

EMPOWERMENT:
The more I honor my truths, the greater my self-worth.

PART FOUR

JUMP

Awakening

This is the game of life. I am Consciousness, incarnate. I've come to this place we call life for a human adventure. The objective is to awaken to who and where I am, by realizing that I've been asleep. If I can stay awake, I win.

Here we are, floating in and around each other's lives. We experience this place, and each other, from within a world of our own. A world confined to overlooked, unexamined and unnecessary thought. Yet we live in the space of endless possibility, where we always have free will to make choices. What and how we choose indicates where we are on this journey back to Self.

Awakening isn't about adding a spiritual label to a personality. It isn't about becoming enlightened and exempt from mediocracy. Awakening isn't about changing your life to get the things the thinking mind wants. What the thinking mind wants is to enhance its identity, and strengthen the box.

Awake, we see our truths. We are able to recognize feel-bad experiences as opportunities for Conscious expansion.

Fear can be embraced as a catalyst for growth and freedom. We have the intrinsic ability to identify unconsciousness and head it off at the pass. One day you will wake up to find that you could do the thing that you could not do. You will suddenly realize that you are not sad, disappointed or angry anymore. You will know peace, beyond the concept.

In lucidity, we find our purpose, and begin to become our true Self. We recognize that there is no truth in anger, hurt or sadness. We discover that we are able to step out of pain and suffering. We realize that our misunderstandings are blameless, shameless, guiltless. We are innocent. We are pieces of Divinity, with amnesia, all trying to find our way home.

Waking up to the bigger picture, life as we know it would change. We would not go to war to cripple each other in an attempt for ultimate control. We would no longer perpetuate conflict at the expense of the masses. We would no longer be slaves to the illusion. We will begin to create a new world.

It's time to evolve beyond the self-made identity, and to awaken into that which we really are. It's time to go beyond the concepts, into higher intelligence. It's time to start living in peace, abundance and joy, individually and globally. It's time to awaken and live authentically.

New World

We are living at a time of evolutionary change. We are on this ride at a minute to midnight. We will either awaken, or it's likely we will experience a rough ride. It's time to change our minds about a few things. Our evolution depends on it.

The world as we know it, was built on a paradigm that does not serve everyone. History suggests that this is a system that serves the few, at the expense of the many, and at the expense of the environment. War, poverty and the myth of scarcity are key elements in this antiquated formula. A new day is built on a new paradigm.

There's only one way to authentically change the world. We each have to clean our own backyard. I'm ready to take responsibility for allowing myself to believe what I'm told without questioning it. I'm ready to admit that I have fallen for the smoke screen that is the promise of making the world a better place, without changing the paradigm. I'm ready to take an honest look at myself to discover the false beliefs that do not serve.

Are we to go forward to build and rebuild without first upgrading the foundation? Am I supposed to chase abundance while I'm programmed to believe in scarcity? Am I supposed to work hard to uphold a system that perpetuates unconsciousness? This is why the Universe taps me on the shoulder with fender-benders and unprecedented Frankenstorms. It's telling me that it's time to wake up.

Creating a new world must be done from lucidity, not from unawareness. In an awakened world, we could continue to enjoy technological advancement, at the same time that every sentient creature has a safe home and clean water to drink. We could continue the exploration of outer space, from a planet no longer plagued with people dying in anguish from lack of medical attention or sustenance. Recreating the paradigm from an awakened state of being, will result in a world where everyone thrives, and does not have to fight to survive.

Everyone deserves the opportunity to pursue their dreams and to fulfill their life purpose. Everyone.

The good news is that we don't have to wait. We have the power to change this life experience as we know it. Awakening is like turning on a light. The most we can do as individuals is to turn on our own light. In a dark world, turning on one light at a time, creates a new world. The power is ours. We are finding our power, and learning how to live it.

> *It's not them, it's you.*
> *It's not there, it's here.*
> *It's not then, it's now.*
> *-Author Unknown*

Making The Effort

Waking up out of my own unconsciousness may occasionally take some effort. There may be days when my greatest desire is to give up, and my thinking mind's greatest sorrow is in knowing that I won't. I will make the effort, until I experience the realization that allows pain and suffering to fall away. I will make the effort, until the isness of a situation rises up to wipe the lie of unworthiness out of my eyes. I will make the effort, until truth washes the taste of fear out of my mouth. I will make the effort for an authentic life experience, and a new world. I invite you to do the same. I will stay Awake with you.

EMPOWERMENTS

AT A GLANCE

Practicing The Practice
I have come fully equipped for this adventure. Today I intend to FUEL my life.

Addiction
With each *gem in my basket*, I'm changing my programming, and my life experience. Baby steps get me there.

Anger
I free and empower myself by responding to anger in lucidity, rather than reacting to anger in unconsciousness.

Anxiety
Anxiety is the internal roar of unconsciousness. I witness, accept, flow and awaken.

Attachment
Outside of the fear that is attachment, lies authentic connection, enjoyment, and love.

Bullying
In awareness, I recognize the unconsciousness of a bully. Self-kindness frees me from bullying self, and bullying others.

Change
I flow with the current of life. I accept and rejoice in opening the gifts of change.

Creativity
Feel your way through. The muse lives in lucidity.

Control
Being in "control" is being awake, and letting Self lead the way.

Depression
As the lucid eyewitness, I flow unconditionally. I awaken to the bigger picture and turn my ship around.

Desire
I serve my soul, by questioning my desires.

Disconnect
I reconnect to Self and life, by giving my mentally silent, undivided attention. Let the magic begin.

Fear
No matter what fearful movie is showing on the mind's big screen, I am the one in reality, outside of the movie, witnessing it. In reality, I am always okay.

Food
I am greater than my programming. Before every meal and snack, I become the lucid eyewitness.

Forgiveness
They know not what they do. They are unconscious.

Freedom
Awakening is the ultimate freedom.

Future
There's no more powerful way to affect my future, than FUELing my life today.

Gratitude
I venture beyond the concept of gratitude, into the magical experience of it.

Grief
Grief is the messenger sent to remind me to awaken to the connection of eternal love, once again.

Guilt
The story of guilt alerts me to unconsciousness, and the opportunity to facilitate my own evolution.

Happiness
The way to real happiness is in waking up to, and honoring our truths.

Heartbreak
I choose to use my tools to awaken from heartbreak and come back to Self. This too shall pass, and I know the way

Hurt
Reach inside of hurt and learn from it, emerging free and empowered, much like a phoenix from the ashes.

Illness
Illness is a prompting to check my connection to Self. Accept and reconnect.

Inspiration
Letting your gut lead the way, in acceptance and lucidity, opens the door to inspiration.

Joy
In connecting to Self, I connect to, and open the flow of authentic joy.

Life Purpose
Our collective life purpose is to awaken into the bliss of an authentic human adventure.

Loneliness
In self-kindness, and the joys of self-love, there is no such thing as loneliness.

Love
Awakened love is unconditional. I practice unconditional love, for self and others.

Meditation
FUELing my life is the living meditation of authentic living. Plug in and power up.

Money
Money is a reflection of inner thought and belief, and Self is the never-ending source of abundance.

Overwhelm
In peaceful self-kindness, I awaken, refocus, and let it be easy.

Past
I am not the content of my past. I am something much greater.

Peace
Underneath the mental noise, unconditional peace awaits. In lucidity I connect to the peace that I am.

Powerless
In lucidity, power is what I am.

Presence
Presence is the effortless flow of emotion, in unconditional acceptance, while witnessing life in lucidity. Presence is our natural state of bliss.

Problems
Don't shoot the messenger, everything serves. Get lucid, accept, and welcome your truths.

Procrastination
The sign post of procrastination tells me that it's time to FUEL up, and to silently survey my own inner landscape.

Regret
To regret is to lament reality. In acceptance, I remove the painful obstacle of regret and rejoin the flow of life.

Relationships
My relationships are once removed by the filter of thoughts and beliefs. Authentic living makes for authentic relationships, with self and others.

Resistance
Unconditional acceptance eradicates the obstacle and discomfort of resistance, opening my door to limitless possibility.

Sadness
Only in unawareness can I experience sadness. I awaken from the story and reconnect to my power. I choose *for* me.

Scarcity
What I see is what I get.

Shame
I choose to witness thought, flow emotion, and exercise lucidity in unconditional acceptance. These are the self-loving practices that free me from the illusionary prison of shame.

Stress
Stress is a cue to use my tools, and intend and allow it to be easy. My balanced well-being is in the highest good of all.

Stuck
I am never so stuck that I cannot reconnect with my power, by surrendering to my own Guidance.

Success
True success is awakening into the bliss of an authentic life experience.

Surrender
In surrender, I allow life to support me in the divine providence of what is.

Vulnerability
The fast track to authentic living and spiritual growth is vulnerability.

Worry
Worry not, for Guidance is always there, pointing me toward my highest good.

Worth
The more I honor my truths, the greater my self-worth.

FUEL
Your Life

A 4-point Practice
To Spiritual Awakening

Written and illustrated by
GINA CHARLES

For more, visit:

GINACHARLES.COM

---

www.ingramcontent.com/pod-product-compliance
Lightning Source LLC
LaVergne TN
LVHW051039080426
835508LV00019B/1606